FAILURE TO LAUNCH

Why Your Twentysomething Hasn't Grown Up ... and What to Do About It

Mark McConville, Ph.D.

G. P. Putnam's Sons
New York

PUTNAM
— EST. 1838 —

G. P. Putnam's Sons
Publishers Since 1838
An imprint of Penguin Random House LLC
penguinrandomhouse.com

Names: McConville, Mark, author.
Title: Failure to launch : why your twentysomething hasn't
    grown up . . . and what to do about it / Mark McConville, Ph.D.
Description: New York : G. P. Putnam's Sons, [2020] | Includes
    bibliographical references and index. |
Identifiers: LCCN 2019021470 | ISBN 9780525542186 (hardcover) |
    ISBN 9780525542209 (epub)
Subjects: LCSH: Parent and adult child. | Adult children living with
    parents. | Young adults. | Adulthood.
Classification: LCC HQ755.86 .M3985 2020 | DDC 155.6/59—dc23
LC record available at https://lccn.loc.gov/2019021470
p.   cm.

Printed in the United States of America
10 9 8 7 6 5 4 3 2 1

Book design by Katy Riegel

Dedicated to my children,

Luke Francis and Meghan Hayes,

and to my brothers, John, Paul, and Mike

Author's Note

In my practice as a clinical psychologist over the past four decades, I have seen hundreds of individuals, including adolescents and young adults and their parents. This book draws in particular on my experiences with patients (both transitioners themselves and their parents) struggling with adolescent-to-adult transitions. Their stories are an invaluable part of this book not only because readers may see aspects of their own or their children's experiences in the fact patterns, but also because their stories have immutably shaped and informed my work and my treatment philosophies. The reader should note that in order to disguise my patients' identities, I have created composites, and have changed names and distinguishing details. However, the issues, dilemmas, and scenarios described herein are all realistic, true-to-life depictions of the developmental issues, parenting challenges, and counseling strategies that flow through my office daily. The reader should also note the inherent limitations of my case studies, which reflect the actual client population of my private practice: more male than female; more middle and upper middle class than otherwise; and while it may not be evident on the printed page, more Caucasian than minority. These limitations are what they are, and I want to acknowledge them.

Throughout the book I offer suggestions for dealing with specific transitioning issues and scenarios, but as is always true in life, there is no one answer, approach, or method that will work for everyone. My approach is intended as parent guidance for normative developmental tasks, challenges, and crises, but not as intervention for clinical mental health issues. All of my clients were working hand in hand with a mental health professional (me), and readers should consider doing the same when there are questions of mental, emotional, or behavioral health. My recommendations are not medical or clinical psychological advice, and you should not implement any strategies without first consulting your healthcare practitioner. I have included them because I believe the best patient is an educated patient—the more informed you are, the better you will be able to collaborate with your doctor to come up with a treatment plan that suits your or your child's individual needs. The appendix provides suggestions and guidelines for seeking professional help for yourself and/or your transitioner.

Contents

PART III

FAILURE TO LAUNCH

Part I

Where Are the Adults?

Why Growing Up Isn't What It Used to Be

Chapter 1

Twenty-Two Going on Sixteen

Why Do Some Kids Struggle with the Transition to Adulthood?

Twenty-two-year-old Nick found his way into my office the same way many of my young clients do: as part of a bargain struck with his parents to get them off his back. I'm a therapist who specializes in working with young people and their families, and as Nick sat across from me for the first time, we took the measure of each other. Nick was an attractive guy with a shock of brown hair and an easy smile, but that smile was wary as he began talking.

"I'm here because my mom and dad think I'm a loser," he said.

As a moderately successful high school student in an affluent inner-ring suburb, Nick had once had what seemed like a preordained path in life. High school to college to job, just like his parents. And Nick had tried college. But once he got there, his promising trajectory stalled, turning into a nine-month binge of partying and missed classes. After two semesters, he was placed on academic probation and required to take a leave of absence from university.

Like many young people in similar circumstances, Nick moved back in with his parents, setting up an "apartment" for himself in the basement of their suburban home, ostensibly to ensure his privacy and simulate independence. His parents, initially frustrated and angry with Nick for his college flameout, resigned themselves to his change in status and committed to helping him get his new life on track.

Initially he showed resolve in managing his life responsibly. He was agreeable and helpful, and grateful for his parents' understanding and support. He found a part-time job at a hardware and garden store, which suited his interest in the outdoors and working with his hands. In short order, he was elevated from stocking shelves and loading heavy items to interacting with customers and advising them regarding lawn-care products. His parents were encouraged, seeing this as an indication of initiative and ambition.

By the time I met Nick, however, this was ancient history. The progress in his work life had stalled, as he failed to expand his hours at the store or to find a second job. In evenings after work, he had established a second home at a neighborhood bar, reconnecting with friends from high school and settling in with tavern regulars. Nick often bought rounds for the house, a gesture that elevated his status and offered a sense of belonging in the bar's microsociety.

"It's just like in *Cheers*," Nick confided to me with self-satisfaction.

But while he was finding a sense of connection and belonging at the bar, Nick's relationship with his parents was deteriorating in predictable fashion. Since his work shifts started later in the day, Nick's drinking sessions extended late into the night. With increasing frequency, he came home in various states of inebriation and slept past noon. On occasion, he wouldn't come home at all, spending the night with his girlfriend, also a tavern regular. His "household citizenship" likewise deteriorated, as his demeanor became increasingly reminiscent of the surly sixteen-year-old he had only recently been.

"Honestly, he treats our home like a rooming house," his mother, Renée, confided with exasperation during my initial meeting with his parents, "complete with a stocked refrigerator, kitchen privileges, and full maid and laundry service! He just takes everything we provide for granted."

Nick's parents were good, solid people. His mother went back to work as her children left for college; his father owned and ran a successful small manufacturing business. Both were devoted to the welfare and growth of their children, with an older son approaching college graduation and a younger daughter floating gracefully through tenth grade. But by the time we first met concerning Nick, they were beside themselves with frustration.

Renée was a worrier who couldn't stop herself from trying to be "helpful" in all sorts of ways. She offered suggestions about what Nick might do to improve his prospects and reminded him of opportunities and obligations as they approached. Nick's term for these ministrations was "nagging," and his responses followed a predictable curve of escalating irritability and anger.

Eventually Nick and his parents had a series of ugly shouting matches, the outcome of which was an agreement that they jointly consult a therapist—me.

Nick's father, Seth, was thoughtful and soft-spoken, and his approach to Nick's floundering was man-to-man and business-like. He periodically arranged appointments for the two of them to meet, often over lunch, where he would press Nick regarding his plans for the future while offering ideas and suggestions. These meetings went well on the surface but failed to generate any meaningful change in Nick's behavior. At his best, Nick conceded that his parents were doing their best to be helpful. At his worst, he saw them as intrusive and manipulative.

Seth and Renée's barely concealed agenda was that Nick return to school—where he might learn a trade commensurate with his talents and interests—landscape technology, or turf grass management, perhaps. "We just want to see him doing something that leads to a more promising future," Renée explained. This seemed the logical way for Nick to escape his minimum wage job and the artificial bubble of his tavern-based social life.

In early sessions with me, Nick periodically voiced resolution to move in a constructive direction. In fact, he *had* made some effort to break out of his rut. He had repeatedly asked for more hours at the store, but these were slow to materialize. For the most part, though, his focus was on his parents' attempts to manage his behavior. His attitude vacillated between a subdued concession that he was frustrated with his life and an unpersuasive confidence that he had everything figured out. One week he would discuss (halfheartedly) his plans to research community college associate degree programs, and the next he would criticize his parents for not believing in him. He accepted that he needed to find a way to make and save money, with the objective of moving out, but his resolve was weak, and his words weren't leading to substantial action.

Nick was stalled, and he wrestled with acknowledging it. His life path, just like his involvement in therapy, traced a circular loop of lip service and inaction—heading nowhere.

"This isn't how I thought my son's life would turn out," said Seth. "It's like he's twenty-two going on sixteen. I want him to be financially secure. I want him to have a home of his own. I want him to have a partner and a family of his own someday.

"But first I have to get him out of my basement."

■ ■ ■

What are parents in situations like this to do? How should I, as a therapist, advise Seth and Renée? Meeting them in my office, I encountered two caring and resourceful people who were willing to do almost anything if it would help their son escape the rut he had created for himself. But they were between a rock and a hard place. Every tactic they tried—urging, cajoling, hinting, suggesting, supporting, guiding—was met with increasing irritation, conflict, and emotional distance.

Should they be *more* emotionally supportive of Nick, given that he was experiencing his own frustrations? Unfortunately, it seemed like the more sympathetic they were, the *less* Nick was motivated to advocate for himself. Their empathy appeared only to soften Nick's resolve.

Should they draw a line and refuse him further support? They considered this strategy, knowing in their hearts that something like this might eventually become necessary. But where would he go if they kicked him out? They feared—with good reason—that removing him from their orbit entirely would decrease their opportunity to exert influence, driving him to become even more entangled with his "going nowhere" social circle.

Seth and Renée's experience is devastatingly familiar to many of us. We love our children so much, we see such incredible potential in them, and we desperately want them to succeed. Yet they struggle to find their way in the world, and we're not sure how to help them. When they were small, we could ground them or withhold a privilege to get them to behave. But once a child becomes an adult (defined as eighteen in most states), relationships with parents become, at least legally, voluntary on both sides.

We are continually trying to redefine our relationships with these adult children—who are sometimes living under our roof, sometimes taking our financial help, and sometimes making what we consider to be poor decisions. What is our role in their lives? How much should we help them? How hard should we push them? We're committed to providing our kids with the help they need, yet we often lack sufficient access or leverage to influence their development. We still have all the guilt, all the anxiety, all the pressures of being a parent . . . but we no longer have the power to enforce, well, *anything*.

I'm here to tell you: You're not alone. A whole generation of parents and kids is dealing with these same issues. But why? Why are more kids than ever struggling with the transition into adulthood? How do we parent an adult who still acts like, as Nick's dad said, he's "twenty-two going on sixteen"?

The Failure to Launch Syndrome

In my private psychology practice, I've worked with hundreds of young adults and their families, grappling with just these issues. Kids who are having a hard time getting a foothold in their adult lives. Parents who feel helpless to assist them. Families strained to the breaking point by these conflicting pressures. This phenomenon has become so common that many clinicians call it failure to launch syndrome.

(If you're wondering: Yes, the name is a nod to the 2006 movie in which a pair of desperate parents hire Sarah Jessica Parker to wrangle their ne'er-do-well son, Matthew McConaughey, to move out of their house. And no, to the best of my knowledge, this has never worked in real life. Hence this book.)

Why is failure to launch syndrome even a *thing*? One reason: Today's parents stay engaged in their twentysomethings' lives much longer than parents in previous generations. In fact, a recent study by the Pew Research Center found that a third of today's twenty-five- to twenty-nine-year-olds live with their parents—three times as many as in 1970. A host of factors account for this change. For one, it's harder today for a twentysomething to earn an

9

independent living, as real wages have dipped and housing costs have risen gradually over the past half-century. Often the childhood bedroom at mom's or dad's is the only affordable option. On top of that, the educational requirements for today's workforce, compared with that of the manufacturing economy of yesteryear, are considerable—and expensive. Education requires financing, and financing requires, in most cases, parents.

As if all this isn't enough, there has also been a massive change in our culture's norms around sex and marriage. For centuries, marriage was the most reliable catapult for launching twentysomethings from cohabitation with and financial dependence upon their parents. But beginning with the cultural revolution of the 1960s and 1970s, sex outside of marriage became a nonissue for most people, and marriage is no longer a certainty. In 1960, 70 percent of the adult population was married, and an unmarried thirty-year-old was socially suspect. Today, just 50 percent of the adult population is married, and the median age of marriage has shifted from the early to late twenties. It's no wonder more and more post-high-school and post-college twentysomethings live at home with mom and dad.

But more underlies this phenomenon than just the economic realities of today's world, the changing educational requirements for today's workforce, and the evolving cultural norms for being regarded as an adult. There's something *underneath* the surface, something harder to measure.

At the heart of much of this failure to launch phenomenon is anxiety. Young people today are more anxious than generations past about leaving behind the supportive framework of parents to take the leap into what's next . . . and some of that is due to the parents themselves. (*Ourselves,* I'll say—I'm also a parent of two.) Today's eighteen-year-olds have grown up in a world largely overseen and managed by adults—in school, of course, but also in after-school programs, sports teams (as well as sports camps and skill-development programs), youth theater, music programs— the list of adult structured activities and avocations for today's youth is exhaustive. This means that today's high school graduate, however much he or she complains about the overinvolvement and micromanagement by adults in his or her life, continues to rely on that involvement and management.

According to some high-school-based college counselors with whom I've spoken, this often leaves students at high school graduation less prepared for the transition into adulthood than their peers from previous generations. They may be well prepared *academically,* but they are more reluctant to take ownership of their lives, more intimidated by the post-high-school world (whether college or full-time employment), and more sensitized to the possibilities of rejection and failure.

In short, they worry more and risk less.

We get the same picture from college mental health services. Students of previous generations would have been hard-pressed to find the mental health services on college campuses. Today these services are flooded; in many instances, it can takes weeks to get an appointment for a nonemergency situation.

When I began my clinical practice in adolescent and family psychotherapy decades ago, the mantra for professionals like me, working with teenagers, was "We've just got to get him or her to age eighteen!" Why? Because back then, conflict with parents typically diminished significantly as age eighteen and high school graduation approached, when the "real world" of necessity took over the job of "parenting." A therapist's task was difficult—because adolescents can be challenging—but also simpler. Because if we could get them to control their impulses just a bit, exercise a modicum of judgment, stop momentarily to anticipate consequences, take school a little more seriously, cut back on alcohol or pot, learn how to lessen conflict with parents—they could arrive at age eighteen intact and ready to launch. The realities and necessities of the post-high-school world would take over from there.

And that's what happened, most of the time.

But something changed.

In the mid-1980s, when the UCLA Higher Education Research Institute began asking first-year students if they "felt overwhelmed by all I had to do," less than 20 percent answered in the affirmative. By 2010, that number was almost 30 percent. In 2017—just seven years later—it jumped to more than 40 percent.

My private practice saw a similar jump, as I received more and more referrals for clients in the eighteen- to twenty-five-year-old age range who presented *not* with adult therapeutic issues ("I'm anxious or depressed . . . was jilted in a romantic relationship . . . am unhappy with my job . . .") but with *adolescent* therapeutic issues—fighting with parents, failing in school, lacking direction and initiative, avoiding and evading responsibilities. These young-adult clients were presenting with problems I would have expected them to have already outgrown. Twenty-two going on sixteen, indeed.

And their parents were stuck in this adolescent limbo, too! These well-meaning souls typically found themselves in an impossible situation. They were unable to withdraw support from a struggling and underprepared twentysomething child, but they were also learning that strategies they'd used for parenting an adolescent—setting clear limits, arranging consequences, limiting privileges, having heart-to-heart talks—were not only ineffective but often counterproductive for their older child.

Why Do Some Kids Struggle with the Transition to Adulthood?

As Seth and Renée found, effectively parenting young people who are having difficulty in their transition into adulthood—I call them *struggling transitioners*—is challenging. It requires an open mind, a big heart, and a willingness to change your assumptions and approach.

These kids aren't lazy. They aren't unintelligent, either. Some of the smartest young people I've met are struggling transitioners. But the common denominator among all of them is that they lack key skills that will help them make the leap from adolescence to adulthood. Skills like administrative responsibility (paying bills, making appointments, meeting deadlines) or the cultivation of interdependence (knowing how and when to constructively ask for help—like when you need to open a bank account, make a budget, or understand a lease) are key aspects of, as the kids call it these days, "adulting."

But most kids don't just pick these skills up by osmosis.

A word to you, the parents, here. Some of this is going to be hard to read. Maybe these are things you think you should have taught your child earlier. (It's okay; we're not going to play in the blame game in this book.) Perhaps they are skills that you have tried in vain to instill in your child for years. (We'll talk about alternative strategies.) And I'm not going to pretend that this work will magically transform your family overnight. But once struggling transitioners start to understand what skills they need in order to take the next steps in their lives and, crucially, *why* mastering these skills is the key to more happiness and success, they can become partners in (and even leaders of) their own futures.

I've seen it happen time and again.

So how do I tackle this problem with the families I work with? Over the last forty years, I've developed a philosophy of parent support and guidance, as well as a specific methodology of getting to the heart of what's really stalling a young person's development. When parents consult a child development specialist, their understandable wish is to be told how to resolve a perplexing and difficult situation. On occasion—particularly when the problem is familiar and straightforward—I do exactly that: I tell people what need to do.

When a four-year college or university student has come within a hairbreadth of failing out or saved his academic skin by virtue of withdrawals and incompletes, parents often ask if they should send the student back for the following semester. I have a fairly standard reply: "You can do that or you can take that tuition money up to the casino. Your odds of success are about the same."

My guidance is pretty straightforward: full-time work for at least a semester, and two community college courses successfully attended, navigated, and completed. Don't take the gamble (and it's *always* a gamble) of sending him back to school until he's demonstrated to you that he's a *good* gamble: He gets up and gets to work every day and can manage the basic responsibilities of being a student.

But in the majority of situations, it's not that simple; pointed advice rarely works as smoothly as the advice giver imagines. Dr. Phil and other media personalities seem to pull it off week after week on television and radio, but for the majority of real-world parent consultations, an in-depth and multidimensional approach is required.

In my work with parents of struggling transitioners, I set three objectives that I know will put them in a better position to help their children.

The first is helping parents acquire a better understanding of the "inner world" of growing up. Why are these young people struggling? What challenges are they facing? When we encounter transitioners who are stalled and struggling with the challenges of adulthood, we inevitably encounter behaviors that don't quite make sense or seem irrational from an objective, common-sense point of view. If there's one thing I have learned in my years as a parenting consultant, it's that it's difficult to help a child get unstuck if we don't understand what's holding that child back in the first place. In Part I of this book, we'll look at the new science of adolescent and young adult development to better understand why young people today are struggling to make this transition in ever greater numbers.

The second objective for parents of struggling transitioners is to understand the three key developmental challenges that young people need to master in order to make better decisions and chart their own paths in life. These are the "adulting" skills I referenced earlier. Specifically, these are becoming responsible (chapter 4), becoming relational (chapter 5), and becoming relevant (chapter 6). For some teens, these skills come naturally; they may seem wise beyond their years or may have been responsible and self-directed from an early age. Other young people need to consciously work on and develop these skills. In Part II, we'll explore in depth what these skills are and start to suggest how parents can cultivate them in their children—even if those "children" are twentysomethings living in their childhood bedroom.

The third objective—the subject of Part III—is helping parents establish a working set of guidelines and principles for making critical parenting decisions. When and how should you provide support? When and how should you draw the line? When should you reach out and when should you hold back? When should you intervene and when should you allow consequences to play themselves out? These are day-to-day dilemmas for parents, who often find themselves flipping mental coins to make these decisions, or repeating interventions that have proven themselves ineffective or counterproductive. This third objective—knowing what to do and when—depends upon understanding why your transitioner is stalled, stuck, and scared in the first place. Part III walks parents through their own sets of challenges, as well as tasks they must master to help their struggling transitioners grow up.

A Word to Parents

If you've picked up this book, I have a pretty good idea how you're feeling about your struggling transitioner, and how shaky and confused you may be feeling about your options as a parent. You and I haven't met in person, but in a very real sense you've come to my office hundreds of times. I know all about the academic flameouts, the missed appointments, the phantom "job searches," the irritable snapping when you simply ask about his plans for the future. I know about the alcohol use and abuse, about the daily pot smoking, and also the opioid and heroin addiction that has you too terrified to sleep at night. And the diagnoses—ADHD, depression, bipolar disorder, just to name a few—which may clarify some of what you're faced with, and also may just add to the confusion. I know how that works, too.

I know how overwhelming all this can seem.

If you've turned to mental health professionals, I hope you have found them helpful. But I've talked to many families who have not. Full disclosure: I'm a huge believer in the value of psycho-therapy; that shouldn't surprise you. But therapists are inclined to utilize an intervention model based upon the *chronological* age of their client, rather than their *developmental* maturity level. In prac-tice, this means that parents such as yourself are often shut out of the therapy process while their struggling transitioner participates in merry-go-round therapy: round and round, getting off exactly where they got on.

I learned years ago that for me to help struggling transitioners, I had to recruit their parents into a working partnership. Once parents examined and reorganized their parenting in the ways I'll discuss throughout this book, my job as their child's therapist be-came much easier—and much more productive.

Think of this book as a partnership. I'm inviting you into my office, just as you're inviting me into your family's life. I'm going to teach you what I've learned about intervening effectively with kids like yours. I'm not suggesting it's easy—quite the contrary. But I am telling you it's *possible*!

Parents should know:

■ More twentysomethings than ever are struggling with the transition to adulthood as a result of more parental enga-gement (aka helicopter parenting), a more challenging economic environment (making it harder for twentysome-things to strike out on their own), and big changes in cul-tural norms (delaying marriage and other "traditional" harbingers of growing up).

- Kids today worry more and risk less—there are huge increases in anxiety and depression among young people today.
- For all these reasons, young people aren't mastering the three critical challenges of emerging adulthood: becoming responsible, becoming relational, and becoming relevant.
- All this to say, you're not alone, parents! In order to help your kids, you need to understand what these new developmental stages are, what challenges young people today will face, and how you can help them move through them.

Chapter 2

Is There Life After High School?

The First Big Transition in a Young Person's Life

E arly one spring morning at my office, I opened a panicky email from the mother of eighteen-year-old Kyle, a high school senior and therapy client of mine. Kyle refused to go into school that day; his mother asked if I would give her a quick consultation by phone. I called immediately and asked if she would put Kyle on the phone.

"I can't," his mom replied.

"Why," I asked?

"Because he's on the floor under his bed, and he won't come out."

Kyle was in the throes of what I have come to call senior year collapse, an acute loss of initiative and motivation, coupled with episodes of overwhelming anxiety. I see this more often than you'd expect, often from previously high-achieving or at least solidly performing students who suddenly change behaviors as graduation approaches. The result is senioritis on steroids—a complete work stoppage and a stubborn retreat from anything connected with preparation for the future, as if the individual were trying to stop the progression of time itself. Senior year collapse is its own unique phenomenon, different from the psychiatric disorders of clinical depression and generalized anxiety. There's no suicidal thinking, and if the situation involves anything other than school, the individual functions just fine.

When I first met with Kyle, he agreed with his parents that he needed outside help. When I inquired about his reasons for coming, he cited lack of motivation in school. Kyle assured me he understood the importance of education and intended to attend college upon graduation. He was bright, according to standardized testing scores, but he was becoming increasingly concerned with his inability to overcome "laziness" (his word). He was, as he put it, a "last-minute guy," procrastinating until a project was due, and then with the deadline looming and often with parents or teachers breathing down his neck, completing the task only at the last minute.

When his English teacher assigned their first real term paper and structured the project in a series of sequential component tasks, each with its own deadline, Kyle blew off the entire series and wrote a fifteen-page paper the night before it was due. "I got a B," he stated with evident pride, "and it would have been an A if I'd done everything according to the teacher's schedule." When he fell behind in turning in chemistry lab reports, he caught up only after his teacher emailed his parents, who then placed him under house arrest until the missing reports were completed.

"I've got to find a way to get myself motivated," Kyle said with genuine concern and exasperation.

"But you already have," I replied.

He looked at me quizzically. "Wait . . . what? What are you talking about?" he asked.

"You have actually worked out a fairly elaborate 'motivational system,'" I pointed out. "And for all the hassle and stress it causes you, it actually works! I mean, in the end, the assignments do in fact get done. You haven't been held back a grade for not doing the work. You actually have pretty decent grades, and with your super SAT scores, are likely headed to a pretty good college. So, yeah, you've worked out a system, and your system works."

The one glaring problem, however, is that Kyle's system relied on the *environment* to supply the energy. Had he attended a large, understaffed public high school, he probably would have fallen through the cracks by now. But he attended a wonderful private school, where there were sheepdogs galore to nip at your heels and get you back on track.

I looked him squarely in the eyes. "But *you* know—we *both* know—college is going to be different," I said to him. "And your system is going to break down."

Kyle, like most high school seniors, had begun to sense the winds of change. He knew that college would be different from high school, *and* that his way of doing business was not going to cut it in the future. It was time to grow up, but he was nowhere near ready.

A New Definition of Growing Up

What do we mean by *growing up*? It's one of those expressions that have become a part of everyday discourse. No one ever stops and asks, "What do you mean by that?" when you tell someone your twentysomething has become "a real grown-up," or when you observe that an old college friend has "never really grown up." But do we really understand what *growing up* means?

Psychologists are starting to understand that the lines between adolescence and adulthood are blurred, and that the demarcation between being a kid and being a grown-up isn't always as clear as we've often thought it to be. Dr. Jeffrey Arnett of Clark University in Massachusetts is a leading researcher of this age group. He asked young people between the ages of eighteen and twenty-nine what it takes to make a person feel like a grown-up. As their three top criteria, they identified "to accept responsibility for yourself," "to make independent decisions," and "to become financially independent." Most of us would probably agree with this assessment. These accomplishments are the crucial signals that a young person is indeed transitioning from adolescence and working through the developmental tasks that lead to adulthood.

When we view this developmental transition from the outside, it comprises a relatively straightforward to-do list: prepare for the future, take on the beginnings of financial self-support, accept responsibility, stop acting like a teenager, and so on. Most of us accomplished this more or less successfully—and in retrospect it may not seem like all that big a deal, this business of growing up.

It's because growing up *seems* like such a straightforward and natural process that we are left scratching our heads, wondering what the problem is for transitioners like Nick and Kyle. If we're going to make sense of their difficulties, we're going to have to take a closer look at the developmental process that we casually label *growing up.*

Developmental psychologists view human development and the life cycle as a progression of relatively stable periods punctuated by destabilizing transitions. And many experts are of the opinion that the transition from adolescence to adulthood is the most destabilizing of all. The adolescent's job is to distance him- or herself from the psychological environment of childhood (namely, home and parents) and to establish a norm of semi-independence in the peer culture of high school society. It's why your formerly clingy kid no longer wants anything to do with you!

Developmental transitions are times of change and reorganization, during which the ground rules of thinking, behaving, and relating are redefined. During these transitions, the roles individuals assume, the norms against which they are judged, the adaptive skills required, and the expectations coming from the environment are all recalibrated, and sometimes redefined altogether. For the transitioner, in other words, there is a *paradigm shift* in the individual's fundamental experience of self and world.

For most eighteen- to twenty-two-year-olds, the adolescent agenda fades and is replaced by a more serious interest in the future, or at least a commitment to preparing for the future. This is what college, the armed services, and an individual's first full-time employment are all about. For the majority of those in their late teens and early twenties, this transition happens more or less quietly, at least at the level of outwardly observable choices and behaviors. For others, like Nick and Kyle, who find themselves overwhelmed and underprepared for the curriculum of growing up, the transition can be a time of turmoil and crisis.

Getting a Life

Have you heard the everyday expression "Get a life"? As in "He needs to get himself a life," or "I have a wonderful life," or "I hate my life?" What does *a life* mean in this context? It turns out this colloquial expression has a scientific basis. The concept of *life structure* was first introduced in a landmark study of development by the psychologist Daniel Levinson in 1978. It's a helpful idea for making sense of struggling transitioners like Nick and Kyle, who seem suspended in a limbo between the different life structures of adolescence and adulthood.

To understand Levinson's concept of life structure, think first of the "self," or personality, as the core organizing principle of any individual's psychological makeup. My "self" is who I am, and includes everything that psychologically defines and identifies me as a unique individual. It includes my sense of purpose in life, my goals and values, my motivational patterns, my interpersonal style and relationships, my identity, and everything else that makes me who I am. Commonsense psychology tells us that the self is something we carry around inside ourselves, something that travels with us when we move from place to place, from job to job, from relationship to relationship, or from one developmental stage to the next.

But psychology has come to realize that this commonsense notion—what psychologist Gordon Wheeler calls the "self-in-isolation" model—is largely a fiction. In fact, one's self is always embedded in a complex scaffolding of relationships, environments, involvements, commitments, goals, values, and activity patterns that give daily life its form and substance. This web of involvements and commitments is what Levinson calls our life structure, and it includes the people, places, things, and interests that form the texture of our day-to-day lives.

My own life structure includes my relationships with my wife and children, as well as with colleagues and friends, my place in my extended family and my professional community, the office I go to most days, my working relationship with my clients, the hardware store I visit some Saturday mornings, and so on. If somehow this world of mine were turned topsy-turvy or began to fall apart, my sense of self—which includes my self-concept, my self-esteem, my self-confidence—would lose its coherence and solidity. All of these things—the personal and professional relationships, the interests and beliefs, the activities and goals—act like so many guy wires anchoring me to this thing I call my life.

The reason this concept of life structure is so important is that the primary task of the post-adolescent transition is the dismantling of an old life structure of childhood and the construction of a new adult one in its place. This is precisely the task that has stalled Nick and Kyle in their tracks. Their unreadiness for the transition shows itself in their avoidance of future planning, their perpetuation of adolescent behavior patterns, and their reliance on conflict with their parents to deflect from the challenges of emerging adult responsibility.

High School as a Life Structure

The adolescent self is anchored in the life structure of high school. Toward the end of high school, we hope to see the emergence of a more mature, adult-oriented self, whose life structure is reorganizing around the project of preparing for eventual entry into the adult world. Not surprisingly, the ending of high school—twelfth grade in the United States—brings with it the winds of developmental change, and it ushers in the beginning of the transition from adolescence to adulthood. Twelfth grade is only the beginning of a years-long process, but it offers us a unique perspective on each individual's readiness to begin the journey. It's a year of psychological sea change, and a closer examination of its developmental agenda will help us in understanding the successes and the failures, the progress and the stalling out, that unfold in the years that follow.

Now, anyone who has experienced a high school senior firsthand knows that they can be mercurial creatures. Some days you look at your child and see a full-grown adult. The next moment, you glimpse the gawky kid again. This is completely normal.

Typically, senior year in high school reveals an overlapping of adolescence and emerging adulthood, as twelfth graders continue to invest energy in holding their parents at arm's length and actively resist what they experience as control and micromanagement by adults. At the same time though, most high school seniors continue to depend upon adults, as they initiate plans for their post-high-school existence, meeting with college counselors, approaching teachers for letters of recommendation, looking for part-time work, and so on.

Senior year in high school is probably the ideal laboratory for understanding the developmental tension between the familiar life structure of adolescence and the beckoning life structure of emerging adulthood. This is not to say by any means that this transition is completed in the senior year. It's just that in the senior year of high school we often find remarkably clear manifestations of the tension, confusion, and ambivalence that attend this transition out of adolescence and into the next phase of life. It's the first time young people have to rethink their self and start to imagine a new life structure for themselves after high school. And for many of them, it's scary as hell. As a result, many kids struggle at this stage—even kids who have seemingly done just fine for most of their school careers.

Kyle was locked in just such a struggle. In his case, it was manifested in his inevitable procrastination where schoolwork was involved. Procrastination is an interesting phenomenon, representing a sort of compromise between warring factions in the procrastinator's psyche. One part of Kyle recognized the importance and necessity of doing the work and preparing for his future. Another side dug in its heels and refused to go along, holding on to adolescence for dear life. The first position was clearly and consciously expressed: "I *need* to get this done. It's *important*. It's *necessary!*" The resistant adolescent force was more *felt* than consciously articulated: "This is *boring*! I *don't want* to do it."

In procrastination, these two parts of self get together in what is more like a wrestling match than a conversation and arrive at a negotiated compromise: "Okay, I'll do it . . . but I'll do it *tomorrow!*" That's the essence of procrastination, in a nutshell.

It's interesting to note that for Kyle, as is the case for many young people struggling with the transition toward adulthood, ambivalence and procrastination became a problem only with endeavors specific to preparation for the future, like schoolwork. In other endeavors, no such conflict emerged. For example, Kyle was the sports editor of his school newspaper, which required him to marshal his resources and meet deadlines, which he did with impressive competence. Sports, for Kyle, was an amusement, an indulgence. Schoolwork was about growing up.

Is There Life After High School?

So what's a kid like Kyle to do? The transition out of high school is so intimidating for some young people that they avoid it entirely. Others, like Nick (from chapter 1), drift along through high school but freeze entirely when faced with the different, and often more self-directed, demands of college. When I refer to high school, I don't just mean a building with books and teachers and classrooms, of course. I'm referring instead to the organized psychological *world* that most adolescents in developed nations inhabit, the underlying *life structure* that gives the adolescent self its sense of meaning, direction, purpose, and identity. In senior year, as the end of high school approaches, this world begins to lose its coherence; it begins to fall apart. There are multiple ways this world begins to dismantle itself.

The first winds of change often announce themselves in the chorus of new expectations that rises from the wider social world. "What are your plans?" most of us reflexively ask when we encounter a high school senior, in almost any social situation. And indeed, for the late adolescent, it is very much like a chorus. It comes from parents, from aunts and uncles, from teachers and guidance counselors, and from peers as well. Particularly for those who feel unprepared and unready (something I'll speak about at length later on), this chorus of expectations has an ominous and frightening quality.

In my counseling work with this age group, I have many times encountered individuals who admitted to a nearly phobic avoidance of certain social gatherings, simply because the inevitable questions about their plans for the future made them so uncomfortable. Similarly, many who feel this way concoct a sort of canned answer or brief "stump speech" to deflect the issue from serious consideration.

"I'm going to work for my uncle in California," one of my clients would routinely say, though he barely knew the uncle in question and had not taken any concrete steps to explore the possibility. Avoidance and deflection in the face of society's changing expectations are not at all uncommon.

These changing expectations are reinforced by the official change in legal status that comes with being a legal "adult"—which, in most places, happens at age eighteen. Behavior that might previously have been considered simply a neighborhood prank or a schoolyard scuffle now has the potential of being regarded as a criminal act. One eighteen-year-old high school client of mine, while visiting his older brother at college, was confronted by campus police while urinating against a building after a night of college partying. A year earlier he might have received nothing more than a stern talking-to. But in this instance, it required serious legal support from his parents to prevent him from being labeled a sexual offender. Such is the considerable vulnerability of being defined legally as an adult.

Perhaps most significant, the relationship of an eighteen-year-old with his or her parents changes at a bedrock level, in that the relationship now becomes *voluntary* on both sides. No one—neither the parent nor the transitioner—is *required* to stay engaged. Parents could decide unilaterally to suspend their support and even kick their child out to fare for him- or herself at any time. (Most don't, but the option is there.) And transitioners, should they choose, could leave the family circle on a whim. And even though this revision of the underlying ground rules usually goes unspoken, it is intuitively understood that change is necessary. Families like Nick's, who remain entangled in the relational dynamics of adolescence well past the teen years, feel this necessity to change, but they are ensnared in the unfinished developmental business of adolescence.

Most families, by contrast, see their relationships improve after high school graduation. Typical college students are consciously appreciative of the support that their parents provide for their continued education and look forward to seeing their parents when home on breaks from school. They understand, in other words, that their parents are *choosing* to support them, rather than being required to do so. When we encounter exceptions to this rule—young people like Nick who take their relationship with mom and dad for granted—we can be certain that the entire family system is trapped in the adolescent relational paradigm.

The Fear of Freedom

One of the most important changes in senior year has to do with the imminent loosening and withdrawal of adult supervision—something that most high school seniors consciously relish but often unconsciously dread. Keep in mind that the world of high school is in many ways constructed *for* the adolescent *by* the organizing influences of the adult world. Every day, or at least every school day, has structure—places they're supposed to be, things they're supposed to be doing. And even if we take the extreme cases of kids who cut school or don't do a lick of academic work, high school still exists as a framework for day-to-day

33

living. Rebellious teens might even define themselves according to the business of *avoiding* adult oversight and challenging the structures the adult world provides for them. But even this provides their lives with a kind of structure, a set of coherent objectives, and a sense of rebellious purpose, however ill advised.

Many of the middle teens I see in counseling immerse themselves in dedicated games of cat and mouse with their parents and teachers. They sneak out at night, smoke pot or drink alcohol away from adult supervision, copy other people's homework, concoct elaborate cover stories for their adolescent escapades, and so on. This is indeed a game—not in the sense of play, but in the sense of having a set of premises and rules that organize the strategy and objectives of their behavior. The "game" of being a rebellious adolescent is predicated upon the structured "world" of high school—a world with a ready-made map, a playing field on which the lines are drawn for them by adult society. And so even for the teen who regularly flouts the rules, the end of high school signals the impending loss of a familiar and grounding world.

We commonly witness high school seniors actively renegotiating their relationships with the adult world, pressing for greater autonomy and less adult meddling. This is evident at home, where parental authority may be more brazenly challenged or casually dismissed, and where curfews and limits are typically taken less seriously or disregarded altogether. In school communities, seniors often make a point of becoming enthusiastically cavalier concerning school rules and behavior codes. Rule-defying activities such as "senior prank" and "senior cut day" express ritualistically this impulse to throw off the remnants of adult supervision.

Around the time of senior year, the inevitability of impending "freedom" from the organizing life structure of high school begins to feel real for most teens. While this is indeed freeing for most graduating seniors, for many, it also generates a great deal of anxiety. Soon to be left behind are the curfews and niggling "reminders," the exhortations for better time management, and the predictable disapproval of all manner of excess and shortfall. But by the same token, the breathable atmosphere of norms, expectations, and general rules of conduct (which are reassuring for teens in a deep sense, even when they are challenged and ignored) is becoming thinner all the time.

It's Tough to Take Ownership

For procrastinators, those teens who have effectively put their heads in the sand, promising themselves that they'd eventually get around to the preparatory business of getting decent grades or finding a job or making some sort of plan for the real future, time is up. The rent is coming due. That long-postponed future, the one they casually dismissed with fantasies of fame and stardom, or whatever idealized and oversimplified vision of a future they substituted for real preparation (*I was going to become a golf pro!*), comes knocking at the door. It's balloon payment time for the procrastinators.

For twelfth graders with all manner of "issues"—emotional

or learning-related, or just a simple lack of self-discipline—the potency of adult oversight and influence begins to fade. This means that they're about to forfeit all those taken-for-granted outrigger supports that have been keeping them afloat all these years—teachers who nag them about getting work done, parents who make it more difficult to drink or smoke pot as much as they might, or adults who kick them off the computer when they can't tear themselves away.

This was certainly the case for Kyle, the high school senior we encountered at the start of this chapter. His parents and teachers intervened to get him through his school-refusal crisis, paring down his workload, providing him with a tutor, and virtually carrying him across the finish line of graduation. It will surprise no one that Kyle found himself on academic probation at the end of his first year of college, having failed to effect the transition from his environmentally based motivational system to the sort of ownership and self-direction required for successful college performance.

In retrospect, Kyle's senior year revealed that he knew intuitively he was not ready to move on to college, where adult supervision could not be counted on and where robust self-supervision would be required. His senior year collapse was a red flag signaling "I'm Not Ready." It was unfortunate that his adult overseers failed to read that signal correctly and rejected my advice that a delayed high school graduation—or a gap year—would be far preferable to the gamble of his beginning college before he was ready.

Besides the fact that the bill comes due for academic self-management, some graduating seniors have failed to master the tasks of adolescence in the realm of *emotional development*. For these individuals, the prospect of leaving high school behind and moving on to a more independent future can be fraught with ambivalence. Bridie was a classic example of a transitioner who had failed to complete the adolescent developmental curriculum.

When I met Bridie, she was a year out of high school and had recently suffered an acute depressive collapse. Shortly after high school graduation and in an ongoing state of intense conflict with her mother, Bridie left home and moved to another city to share an apartment with her older sister, a medical student. Her stated intention was to find work and support herself, severing all communication with her parents. But full-time employment and financial self-reliance turned out to be more difficult than she imagined, and eight months into her "independence experiment," she was sleeping fourteen hours a day, had stopped showing up for her part-time position as a restaurant hostess, and was severely neglecting basic self-care.

Her parents came and brought her home; she began regular therapy visits with me. I have worked with adolescents and their parents for decades, and the most telling aspect of nineteen-year-old Bridie's therapy was that she and her parents were dealing with issues that were classic for *early* adolescents—years behind where I would have expected their relationship to be.

Younger teens just beginning to differentiate themselves from their parents tend to spend a lot of time quarreling over minor boundary issues relating to privacy and autonomy. For example, Bridie would not allow her mother to do her laundry or to even touch it! Especially her underwear. This behavior is not unusual in a twelve-or thirteen-year-old, but this aggressive rejection of any sort of dependency was not typical behavior for a nearly twenty-year-old. Some key transition had been missed earlier in their relationship, and Bridie's therapy resembled a crash course in adolescent development for her *and* her parents.

High school seniors like Kyle and Bridie face a dawning uncomfortable realization that many of the side-rail bumper guards belonging to the world and culture of high school, protections that have been so taken for granted as to be almost invisible, are soon to be removed. Several years ago I sat with a twelfth-grade boy, a mediocre student in a large public high school who was completely flummoxed by the daunting process of applying to colleges.

"What's your strategy?" I asked him. His honesty was disarming, and certainly he spoke for many seniors in the same situation. "Nothing. I'm not going to do anything. Sooner or later my parents will step in. I figure that's how this is going to get done."

The Dismantling of the Social World

What about the great majority of eighteen-year-olds who are, by all objective measures, reasonably well prepared to take the next step? These are the ones who have done the academic work to ready themselves for college or the work world, who are solid high school citizens, who have developed reasonably reliable work habits, and who seem sufficiently competent at managing themselves and their high school lives. They're ready, right?

Well, maybe.

Objectively they are on their way, but they face the same challenges of self-organization as their less prepared counterparts. Their personal worlds are also being remade. They will experience the same painful dissolution of the familiar patterns of daily living that have become, over the preceding years, the scaffolding of their self-knowledge, self-concept, self-esteem, and self-confidence.

All high school guidance counselors and all therapists who work with young people are familiar with the high school senior—the good student, the solid kid, the good citizen—who mysteriously collapses during the final year of high school life. This is the boy who inexplicably stops going to class, or the girl who develops an eating disorder seemingly out of nowhere, or the kid who tumbles unexpectedly into an energy-drained state of anomie, abandoning the college admission process and anything else that works to move him or her forward into the future. These are talented, well-prepared, promising young adults who seem to focus all available energy on the singular mission of stopping time in its tracks. Because, while the adult world may deem them ready, this is not necessarily their own experience.

Among the more painful aspects of the "end of high school" phenomenon is the dismantling of social networks. Think about it: For years, your adolescent has worked hard to find his or her place in high school society. Leaving behind the notoriously unstable social world of middle and junior high school, high schoolers typically find a more secure footing in the world of peers, carving out a niche, a set of attachments, a provisional identity, and a social persona (the "face" in Facebook). This is by no means an easy task, as the unending stream of adolescent social angst movies (*The Last Picture Show, Heathers, Pretty in Pink, American Pie, Juno, Lady Bird,* and so forth) testifies. However difficult and complicated the task of constructing and anchoring a social self during this time, most high schoolers by senior year have found a relatively secure place in the social landscape. They have their friends. They have their identity. But these accomplishments and the psychic stability they help to secure are temporary—and this troubling fact is part of the dawning stress and sadness of senior year.

Sometimes we observe older teens realigning their social connections as they turn their attention toward the business of preparing for their post-high-school years. They may disengage from an earlier adolescent "posse," involve themselves in a serious dating relationship, or form new friendships based upon more mature interests. But in some seniors we also find ample evidence of the exact opposite tendency—an almost desperate clinging to old friends and networks in an effort to preserve the social framework of their identity and emotional equilibrium.

I remember one client who ritualized this process throughout the summer following graduation, as he and his friends anxiously anticipated the departures for college that would deconstruct their social world. Several nights each week, they built bonfires where their extended peer family would gather, sipping beers and reminiscing about the glory days of high school. As the end of summer approached, these meetings felt ever more desperately essential to him. I recall his poignant, if somewhat dramatic, words in a counseling session late in August, when his associates had begun to peel away, and he confided: "I feel like I'm dissolving."

Dramatic, yes. But also in some sense true.

The end of high school is, by its very nature, a developmental crisis. That's the point. In fact, it's an *existential* developmental crisis, meaning that it is a time when the psychological life structure is *necessarily* dismantled, like the circus taking down its tents and packing up, getting ready to move to its next venue. It is existential in the sense that it encompasses a reworking of the very premises of what it means to be a person living a life. Some transitioners—like Nick and Kyle and Bridie—are not ready for this mandate for change and become trapped in a swirling eddy of prolonged adolescence. They experience the dissolution of their high school life structure but are paralyzed by a subjective sense of being insufficiently prepared, frightened by the prospect of launching toward adulthood. Intuitively they understand that it is time to grow up, but don't feel ready, willing, or able to do so.

What is it about *growing up* that makes it so threatening and intimidating to so many transitioners? Maybe growing up isn't as simple as it seems.

Parents should know:

- The end of high school is an existential developmental crisis for many young people—it's the first time they have to renegotiate their sense of self and imagine their place in the entirely new life structure that's to come. Some anxiety and disruption is normal!
- But parents should be concerned if they see red flags like chronic procrastination when it comes to next steps (such as a failure to engage with college or job planning) or serious regression (like failing to keep up with basic self-care or uncharacteristically skipping out on part-time jobs or other responsibilities).
- While many struggling transitioners complain they want more autonomy, many of them actually fear freedom—and if parents don't heed these transition warning signs in high school, they could send to college a child who simply isn't ready.

Chapter 3

When Will I Feel Like an Adult?

The New Science of Emerging Adulthood

On the morning after high school graduation—figuratively speaking—Nick, Kyle, and Bridie woke up in a world asking them to take on a greater degree of self-management, self-regulation, self-direction, and self-support. Overnight they had wandered into the uncharted border region of a foreign territory, familiar landmarks behind them, lacking the map, the guidance, and the resolve necessary to navigate their way. Their notions of what it meant to become a grown-up, insofar as they had such notions, were woefully inadequate.

Bridie thought that getting away from her parents, creating geographical independence, would do the trick. For while she had not in any explicit fashion thought about growing up, she equated adulthood with separation from her parents' influence and control.

For Nick—again, not that he thought about it much—*adulting* meant belonging to an informal fraternity of tavern regulars and being accepted in that environment by people older than him.

And Kyle . . . well, he hadn't given adulthood a minute's thought, committed as he was to avoiding anything that smacked of preparation for the future.

How do we help these struggling transitioners?

My therapy work with Kyle, in the year after his failed college experience, was revelatory of the inner thought processes many struggling transitioners exhibit when they contemplate growing up and feeling like an adult. For starters, Kyle's thinking about these matters—preparing for the future, beginning to imagine what he might become—was conspicuous by its absence. When Kyle shrugged his shoulders and answered, "I have no idea," to simple conversational probes such as "What do you want to *do*?" or "Where do you see yourself five, ten, fifteen years from now?," he was telling the truth. He didn't let himself think about these things.

At all.

This was not a simple lack of interest, in the way that I might not think about, say, chess strategy or dessert recipes—subjects I don't care about. Instead, this was an active, purposeful, and deeply motivated disinterest—the kind of blind spot that protected Kyle from what might otherwise have been overwhelming anxiety.

During our work together, I helped Kyle to come to grips with this avoidance and to begin thinking about his future. And once we began to talk about it, the mystery of his previous avoidance largely disappeared. Kyle's implicit understanding of how the future was "supposed" to unfold, of what his path toward adulthood was "supposed" to look like, was completely wrong. Like so many transitioners with a committed aversion to preparing for adulthood, Kyle imagined the journey in terms that were unlikely, if not altogether impossible.

For one thing, he believed that he was supposed to know *now*, at age nineteen, what he was going to do for the rest of his life. College terrified him, and even thinking about it magnified all the uncertainty and self-doubt in his brain because he didn't know what he was "supposed" to major in. Choosing a course of study had the feel to him of a high-stakes guessing game.

"What if I study something for a few semesters and then just lose interest in it?" he would ask. "What if I find I'm not as smart as people have always told me, after all?"

The conversation I conducted with Kyle over the course of multiple sessions was designed to bring his understanding of how growing up happens, how people find their way from adolescence to adulthood, more in line with reality. It's a conversation I've had, with variations, hundreds of times with young people Kyle's age. This conversation spans many sessions, of course, but if I had to consolidate it into one grand speech, it would go something like this:

"Ask your parents, their friends and colleagues, your former teachers and professors—any adult who seems satisfied and gratified with what they do in life—how they got to where they are. What was their path? You'll find that it's virtually *never* a straight line. It zigzags. It's *supposed* to zigzag. Those adults— you'll find that almost none of them had the faintest idea when they were your age of what they'd be doing now. Your adult future isn't sitting in front of you. It's not in the college major you choose or the job you're about to apply for. It's out there over the horizon. If your thirty-year-old self were to open my office door right now, walk in, and sit down, he'd have a tale to tell that would be full of surprises. Right now, you're Lewis and Clark setting out from St. Louis; you're Frodo just leaving the Shire; you're Luke Skywalker getting ready to leave Tatooine. You can't *possibly* know where you're heading. Your task now isn't to know your destination; it's much simpler than that. Right now your task is to figure out two things: *what you like and what you're good at.* That's what you need to do *now* in order to eventually discover the future you—the one who's waiting out there for current you to find him."

■ ■ ■

The thing that my struggling transitioner clients—kids like Nick, Bridie, and Kyle—almost never understand is that entering adulthood takes time, and that no one is fully prepared when the journey begins. Once I get them thinking about it, I typically ask how long they imagine the process might take. The more realistic thinkers answer along the lines of "five or ten years," which is a pretty good answer. But the truth is that growing up is a lifelong process, something most of us never fully accomplish.

I recently spoke to a group of high school parents and teachers about the challenges of transitioning from adolescence to emerging adulthood, some of the developmental issues we'll look at in Part II. Afterward, no less than half a dozen audience members—high-functioning, successful adults who were all well past their own adolescence—confided to me that *they themselves* were still works in progress, wrestling with the very same issues I discussed.

We're all still growing up a little.

In a similar and somewhat humorous vein, I heard from one of my older brothers recently. This particular brother retired several years ago from a distinguished professional career, and along the way has enjoyed a long and satisfying marriage and raised four vibrant and thriving adult children. When I recently published an article in *The New York Times* titled "How to Help a Teenager Be College Ready," outlining many of the same themes we're discussing in *Failure to Launch,* he sent me a congratulatory note: "Good news: I liked your article. Bad news: I don't think I'm ready for college."

Feeling Like an Adult

In a strictly psychological sense, the transition from adolescence to adulthood is a period of *developmental crisis.* Crisis, by its nature, contains elements of both *danger* and *opportunity.* For most transitioners, it is the *opportunity* that serves as the beacon for their emerging adult development. On the other hand, for those transitioners who struggle and stall in their launch into adulthood, it is the *danger* of the developmental crisis that holds sway. During developmental transitions, we lose the familiar compass points of our previous life structure, and with them, our former sense of security and confidence about what to do and how to go about doing it.

Gail Sheehy referred to these periods as *passages*, noting that they are times of accelerated growth and reorganization, when new challenges are encountered and mastered and new skills and capabilities are developed out of necessity. But these life transitions are also times of heightened vulnerability and uncertainty, when newly required skills and capabilities are still works in progress and very much unproven. Sheehy writes, "With each passage from one stage of human growth to the next, we . . . must shed a protective structure. We are left exposed and vulnerable—but also yeasty and embryonic again, capable of stretching in ways we hadn't known before."

The subjective sense of *feeling like an adult* plays out around behavioral challenges that have obvious importance—being interviewed for a job, signing a lease, or paying bills on one's own. But at the same time, though less obviously, it plays out around behavioral challenges and experiments that seem trivial and incidental, so much so that they are largely invisible to adults.

Virtually everyone, over the long course of childhood and adolescence, develops an unconscious *theory* of adulthood—what it means to be a grown-up. These unconscious theories aren't based so much upon realistic accomplishments such as decision-making and financial self-support as much as they are based upon childhood observations of the subtle trappings of adult status.

Beginning transitioners inevitably experience adulthood as a sort of "foreign territory," an imagined state that has its own norms and standards, its own unwritten criteria for membership, and its own subtle prerogatives and badges. Transitioners typically experience themselves as outsiders who are tentatively and somewhat haphazardly petitioning for apprenticeship and acceptance. They experience boundaries and turnstiles often invisible to the adult eye but which transitioners themselves can be acutely aware of.

I remember buying myself a pair of wing-tip shoes during my first year in college, as wing-tip shoes were an insignia of maturity at the time. I vividly remember my trepidation when I wore them home at winter break my freshman year, wondering if my younger brother would mock me for affecting adult status or whether my parents would simply be amused at my new appearance.

A twenty-one-year-old client of mine related a similar experience of crossing the unmarked boundary of adulthood. He recently sat with his father at an airport bar, waiting to board their flight. "I'd spent plenty of time in airports," he confided, "but sitting at the bar was something *adults* did. I had never done it. I kept having this silly thought that someone was going to come up and tell me I had to leave, that I wasn't supposed to sit there."

On the surface, such private insecurities seem so silly and trivial as to border on the ridiculous. But they aren't trivial at all, insofar as they reflect a deeper *inner world* transformation—a transformation that will lead over time to a solid and abiding sense of *feeling like an adult*.

A New Developmental Stage: Emerging Adulthood

In earlier generations, regarding oneself as an adult was largely a matter of passing certain external benchmarks—completing an education, finding a full-time job, getting married, and beginning a family—all of which tended to happen at a much earlier age than today. According to Dr. Jeffrey Arnett, the leading authority of contemporary emerging adulthood (ages eighteen to twenty-nine), the average age of marriage in 1960 was twenty-two for men and twenty for women. When my generation went to college, there was an implicit expectation that we would meet our future spouses there. And indeed, within a year or two of my college graduation, I and many of my friends were married. Today, the average age of marriage is twenty-eight for men and twenty-six for women—and it's not at all unusual for people to wait until their thirties or later, if they partner up at all.

Again according to Arnett, only 33 percent of people in 1960 went to college, compared to roughly 70 percent today. For those who didn't attend college in the 1960s, well-paying manufacturing jobs were plentiful; for those who did attend college, good jobs or spots in medical, law, or graduate schools were not that difficult to find. Today, Arnett observes, we are shifting from a manufacturing economy to an information and service economy (indeed, that shift is already well under way, and has been for at least a few generations). This means it requires far more education just to qualify for a living wage. For these and a host of other reasons (the sixties and seventies youth movement, the women's movement, the acceptance of sex outside of marriage), growing up today—regarding oneself as an adult—is a longer, slower, evolving process.

Arnett breaks down emerging adulthood into three substages: launching (from eighteen to twenty-two), exploring (from twenty-two to twenty-six), and landing (from twenty-six to twenty-nine). Launching is about leaving adolescence behind and beginning the process of cultivating independence and self-reliance. Going to college, getting a full-time job and taking on the commensurate financial responsibilities, joining the military—all are traditional vehicles for launching toward full-fledged adulthood. The second substage, exploring, is about trying things out, especially in work and relationships. From eighteen to twenty-nine, Arnett tells us, the average twentysomething will have had seven different jobs. Also by age twenty-nine, most individuals have had multiple romantic partners. What finally makes the twenty-six- to twenty-nine-year-old ready to land is the fact that they have accumulated a variety of life experiences, and from those experiences they have learned who they are, what they're capable of, and what they want from life.

When I do an "identity interview" with a twenty-year-old ("So who are you? What really matters to you? What distinguishes you from other people? What are you good at?"), I typically get an intelligent and plausible set of answers. But they are answers based to some extent upon conjecture and speculation. When I do the same sort of interview with a twenty-eight- or twenty-nine-year-old, the answers may seem similar, but they are based upon life experience. The twenties are like a series of internships—all commitments temporary, a series of both intentional and random experiments.

Growing up takes time, as Arnett's research makes startlingly clear. When he asked young people about their *subjective* experience of "feeling like an adult," he discovered that it is not until just past age twenty-six that *half* of his sample reported feeling like an adult, *half of the time*. It takes time, indeed! This is why "holding environments" such as college, structured gap-year programs, and the armed services are so useful and important for growing up, since they allow for necessary skills and capabilities, and the subjective confidence that comes with them, to emerge and solidify over time.

The Tasks Emerging Adults Need to Master

When we encounter struggling twentysomethings like Nick and Bridie and Kyle, what catches our attention are the dysfunctional behavior patterns—the surly attitude, the alcohol abuse, the shaky employment history and financial irresponsibility, the poor academic work habits—behavior patterns that keep them stuck in a developmental freeze-frame. But these behaviors represent only the part of the iceberg that is above water. The real problem is beneath the surface, invisible to the observer and often to the struggling transitioner him- or herself. What I've learned in my many years as a psychotherapist is that the deeper problem lies within, in the individual's *felt sense of self*, a sense deeper than conscious thought and language, of not being ready for adulthood.

How this inner-world transformation comes about—the tasks and challenges that must be faced and resolved in order to make it happen—is the subject of Part II. It's important for us to remember that the *outward* manifestations of growing up— acceptance of real-world responsibility, independent decision- making, and a shift toward financial self-support that Arnett's subjects identified as the hallmarks of adult status—don't just happen. These manifestations of emerging adulthood are what we observe (or in the case of struggling transitioners, what we find so conspicuously missing), but they are the product of a far-reaching curriculum of *inner* psychological growth.

In my years of counseling with struggling transitioners, I have been able to chart this developmental curriculum by not- ing the various ways that young people stall and get stuck, con- fining themselves to patterns of avoidance and denial and trapping themselves in repetitive loops of unproductive "adoles- cent" behavior. The successful transition from adolescence to emerging adulthood involves—underneath the outward behav- ioral benchmarks—an array of important *developmental tasks.* For young people who make this transition without incident, these tasks are undertaken and mastered simply as a matter of course, gracefully and seemingly without special effort. For these young people, the transition virtually escapes our notice. It seems almost as if they are adolescents one day and young adults the next.

For many other transitioners, however, one or more of these tasks requires a bit of psychological work, some encounter with unpreparedness, some initial missteps to be retraced, some learning curve of adaptation and accomplishment. For these individuals, the developmental task becomes a *challenge*. This is probably the norm. Most adults, if we reflect honestly and remember accurately, can recall some aspect of growing into adulthood that caused us to stumble, required a special effort, and involved a significant piece of new learning on our part.

For many of the young people who will appear in the pages of this book, however, one or several of these tasks present sufficient challenge as to impede and stall the developmental process of emerging adulthood altogether, and in these cases the tasks transcend the status of a challenge and become bona fide *crises*.

I have grouped these tasks/challenges/crises under three main headings, each of which will be considered in a chapter in Part II. The first of these is *becoming responsible*, which involves the important business of taking ownership and responsibility for the nuts and bolts of managing one's day-to-day life. What I'll show in chapter 4 is that difficulty with seemingly simple administrative responsibilities (making and keeping appointments, managing bank accounts, paying parking tickets, etc.) can reflect a deeper anxiety about being ultimately responsible for one's life and passing oneself off as an adult.

The second developmental task/challenge/crisis of the emerging adulthood transition is *becoming relational*, which includes a necessary retooling of interpersonal relationships—with peers, mentoring adults, and one's own parents—such that they can provide the various kinds of *support* required for the journey to adulthood.

Finally, the third developmental task/challenge/crisis for all transitioners is that of *becoming relevant* to the adult world, which involves finding a sense of direction and making commitments— to schooling, employment, the armed services, and so forth— that promise (in the face of great uncertainty) a viable path to adulthood.

Although these tasks/challenges/crises are presented here serially, they occur more or less simultaneously, in no particular order. Whether a particular task assumes central importance depends on the unique circumstances, endowment, and psychological history of the individual. It's also important to note that the three sets of tasks are fundamentally interrelated and highly interactive. For many struggling transitioners, one particular task may assume a "keystone" role, setting up problems that roll over into other areas of development and function, creating trouble there as well. In the chapters that follow, we'll consider each of these tasks/challenges/crises in turn, and illuminate the hidden side, the inner world, of growing up.

Parents should know:

- We fail to remember just how foreign adulthood seems for many young people, who may have unrealistic ideas about how growing up happens and may feel woefully unprepared for the process.

- This is partly because we often don't remember the anxiety and uncertainty of our own emerging adult transitions . . . and partly because emerging adulthood (the period from ages eighteen to twenty-nine) doesn't look anything like it once did. Our society and our expectations are still catching up to the new reality.

- For all these reasons, the three challenges of emerging adulthood introduced earlier—becoming responsible, becoming relational, and becoming relevant—take on critical importance and are often the key to moving a "stuck" young person into the next stage of life. In Part II, we'll look at each in turn.

Part II

How to Adult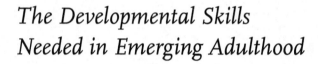

*The Developmental Skills
Needed in Emerging Adulthood*

Chapter 4

Skill 1
Becoming Responsible

*Emerging Adults Must Learn How
to Take Ownership of Their Lives*

I f we needed a one-word definition of what it means to be a grown-up, an adult, that one word would be *responsibility*. Not surprisingly, the most common presenting issue I hear about when meeting with struggling transitioners and their parents is mis- or under-management of responsibilities.

Twenty-four-year-old Zach was a textbook example. Like so many struggling transitioners, Zach had tried college immediately after high school, but he'd made a mess of it. His class attendance was spotty, he managed time poorly, he missed deadlines. When he inevitably fell behind, he avoided his professors and eventually stopped attending class altogether. Zach was definitely bright enough for college-level academics. He had succeeded in high school, but largely thanks to the shepherding of his parents and teachers. In college, however, the requirement to independently manage a schedule and workload seemed beyond Zach's capabilities.

When I met him, Zach was living in a modest, parent-subsidized apartment and working full-time as a ticket taker and lobby attendant at a multiplex movie theater. To his credit, he got to work reliably and on time, and was recognized by his supervisor as a good worker. But even in his success, Zach was worrisomely passive. He went to work only after his parents made it a condition of their continued material support.

In managing day-to-day obligations and responsibilities, Zach exhibited the same patterns he had shown in college. Unlike most transitioners I see in therapy, Zach had few complaints about his life. He was happy with his parents, voiced no dissatisfaction with his occupational status, and verbalized only pipe-dream aspirations for his future (he hoped to be a filmmaker one day). He was pleasant in his interactions with me, but had no real interest in coming to therapy, other than to comply with his parents' insistence that he do so.

In family therapy sessions, I encouraged his parents to turn over certain responsibilities to Zach—like paying his own car insurance and, later, when he had a minor car accident, managing the mechanics of getting estimates and arranging repairs on his own. In my solo work with Zach, I likewise maneuvered to put our relationship on a more adult-to-adult footing. When he missed an appointment and complained that his parents would probably make him pay for it (unfair, he believed, because he didn't want to come to therapy in the first place), I implemented a strategy I often utilize when I'm trying to make therapy feel more like an adult-to-adult relationship: I negotiated a reduced fee for the missed session—one he could afford—and agreed to bill him independently. I believe it's worth the lost income to give my struggling transitioner clients an experience of participating in an adult-world transaction. And it often proves helpful.

Unfortunately, Zach stopped showing up several sessions later, as he remained uninterested and unengaged, and his parents and I eventually agreed that the individual sessions with Zach were not productive. Zach wasn't ready to engage a therapist because, in his experience, his life was going along smoothly enough. Not surprising, he never paid the bill I sent him (his parents later reported that he never even opened the envelope), and his parents made him pay the full fee, just as he had predicted. The car insurance? Mom and Dad had to sit him down and make him write a check in order to prevent the insurance from lapsing. And the car repairs? Not completed when I last met with his parents, who continued to come to me for consultation and support.

What usually happens with kids like Zach—kids whose avoidance of responsibilities more or less "works" for them—is that they don't get interested in outside support until they begin to experience real consequences of their avoidance. I'm waiting to see if that will happen in Zach's case.

But what in the world is going on here? What can possibly account for Zach's failure to manage these simple matters, all of which were in his best interest and well within his capabilities? This is an important question, because learning to manage the mechanics of everyday living is one of the key developmental tasks of transitioning from adolescence to emerging adulthood.

I should note that Zach is not unique, as this sort of mysterious avoidance and neglect of everyday responsibilities is common among struggling transitioners. Let's explore why.

New Paradigm, New Responsibilities

The tasks that struggling transitioners so conspicuously neglect and avoid can be lumped under the general heading of *administrative responsibility*: scheduling and keeping appointments, meeting deadlines, making administrative phone calls, filling out forms, paying bills, attending to license renewals, changing the oil in the car, and the hundreds of other small tasks that constitute the maintenance of a life structure. These are the mandatory details of life—the details that keep life on track, prevent avoidable snafus and crises, and allow the bigger agenda of growth and development to proceed apace.

The very meaning of the word *responsibility* changes over the course of the developmental arc. In childhood, being responsible connotes a sort of dutiful compliance with adult expectations: getting one's homework done without supervision, arriving home on time for dinner, writing thank-you notes for birthday gifts. In other words, when we label a younger child responsible, we mean essentially that he or she is more or less obedient. This is an important trait, and bodes well for a child's growth and eventual adult adjustment.

In adolescence, the psychological meaning of responsibility expands beyond the dutifulness of childhood to include a sense of *ownership* of various commitments and obligations. High school students who responsibly manage schoolwork or practice for music lessons or fulfill an off-season athletic conditioning program aren't simply complying with adult expectations. They are complying with their *own* expectations. They care about their endeavors because they identify with them, and it is through these self-selected commitments that they design and take ownership of their emergent adolescent sense of self.

As we saw in chapter 2, however, even the well-centered, mature, and confident adolescent lives out his or her existence in a life structure that is largely designed, overseen, and monitored by the adult world. But that changes with the end of high school, as the greater portion of the responsibility for preparing and ultimately designing a new life structure shifts from the adult overseers to the transitioner him- or herself. There is, in the transition between adolescence and emerging adulthood, a developmental tipping point of sorts—a shift when the individual recognizes that the adult world, and especially parents, can no longer be relied upon to set the course and manage the direction of one's ongoing development. But what happens when that tipping point simply isn't reached on one's own?

Simply put: Accepting more responsibility can be downright terrifying, and some kids don't want to deal. The transition between adolescence and emerging adulthood finds an individual perched precariously on the developmental watershed between owning a *self* (which is the developmental task of adolescence) and owning a *life* (which is the developmental work of emerging adulthood). Because once we start to take ownership of our lives, then all of it (the good as well as the bad) becomes our responsibility.

The existential psychiatrist Irvin Yalom offers insight into the underlying psychological meaning of responsibility for transitioners. Yalom approaches responsibility from a broad perspective, transcending specific duties and obligations of everyday living, referring instead to the responsibility for "constructing an existence for oneself that has purpose and meaning." Responsibility for the emerging adult, in other words, implies taking *ownership* of one's future. As Yalom points out, a shift of this magnitude and importance cannot occur without significant anxiety—indeed, Yalom labels it *existential anxiety*—at the realization that this life I'm living is truly *mine*, and that ultimately the only thing standing between me and failure is ME!

Yalom writes: "Responsibility means authorship. To be aware of responsibility is to be aware of creating one's own self, destiny, life predicament, feelings and, if such be the case, one's own suffering." The tried-and-true adolescent strategies—simply blowing off obligations and commitments, blaming others for one's difficulties, power-struggling with parents, and unconsciously presuming that adults will somehow keep one's life in order—simply don't work the way they once did. Existential anxiety accompanies the dawning realization that the adult world just isn't buying it anymore.

I myself recall a deeply unsettling moment of this sort during my senior year in high school, at a time when I felt not nearly ready to take ownership of the responsibilities of emerging adulthood. I was wrestling with considerable anxiety over the business of choosing colleges and following through on the concrete particulars of the application process. In those days, parents and high school guidance offices were not nearly as involved in this process as they are today. In the throes of my paralysis, I intuitively—certainly not consciously—opted for a strategy I had nearly perfected in my preceding teenage years, and one that I implicitly trusted would lead to things somehow getting sorted out: I looked for an adult to fight with. Wandering aimlessly and anxiously about the house, not knowing what to do next, I encountered my father—who never disappointed me when I was looking for a fight.

The episode is burned into my memory. My father was sitting reading the newspaper when I approached him and announced summarily, "I think maybe I'm not going to go to college after all!" He looked up from his newspaper and nodded thoughtfully, uncharacteristically silent for a long time. Finally he just said, "Well, then . . ." and went back to reading his paper.

Not what I expected! Absent the showdown, I had to find another way through this sticky situation. I was down at my high school's college counseling office, asking for help with my college applications, within the week.

The Roles of Anxiety and Shame

Remember Zach's mysterious avoidance of simple administrative tasks at the start of this chapter? Why did he do that—and why do so many of us avoid such mundane issues (though perhaps not to such an extreme) in our own lives? This question was answered for me several years ago by twenty-year-old Ben, one of those clients I have come to call "poets" because of their capacity to articulate and make clear the underlying psychological challenges of the emerging adult transition. I had seen Ben in therapy several years previous, at a time when he was fumbling his way through a tumultuous adolescence. He had managed to survive his years of high school impulsiveness and immaturity, had straightened out his relationship with his parents, and seemed by most observable measures to have gotten his life together. He was in college, and while not excelling, he was managing the task of furthering his education and preparing for adulthood.

Ben had just finished his sophomore year and was home for the summer when he phoned. "What's the problem?" I inquired.

"My parents and I are at it again," he answered. But this time Ben was assuming ownership of the situation by taking the initiative to meet with me. And, indeed, the twenty-year-old who arrived at my office seemed far more mature than the sixteen-year-old I had known four years earlier.

The source of recent conflict had to do with Ben's dragging his feet about getting himself a summer job—something his parents required if he was to spend the summer at home. And indeed, Ben *wanted* to work for the summer, but his parents just kept "hassling him" and were "getting in the way" in their overbearing efforts to be helpful.

"I know I have to get a job," said Ben. "I *want* to work this summer! But the first thing my mother says to me in the morning, and the first thing my dad says when he comes home from work, is 'Do you have a job yet?' I swear, they're driving me crazy. I'm *going* to get a job if they would just get off my back."

Once we established that Ben probably didn't have the worst parents in the world, we looked at the possibility that Ben was holding himself back in his job search, somehow getting in his own way. Our conversation eventually zeroed in on his mysterious reluctance to make phone calls to prospective employers. Ben's father had arranged with several business associates to consider his son's application, if only Ben would call and ask for an interview. Ben put the calls on his to-do list daily, but the days dragged on, consumed by all manner of procrastination and diversion, and in the end the phone calls never happened.

Perhaps, given more time, Ben and I would have clarified the mystery of his strange avoidance, and he would have summoned the courage to pick up the phone. What happened instead was that Ben's father, exasperated, preemptively made the calls himself and scheduled the interviews. All of this was accompanied with the bickering and harping and complaining that parents of some twenty-year-olds find disconcertingly familiar.

Ben's behavior raised the same question we encountered with Zach. What in the world was this mysterious resistance about? What could possibly explain such dedicated avoidance of such a simple administrative task? Months later, meeting with Ben prior to his return to school, I unexpectedly tripped across the explanation for his curious, if not uncommon, avoidance and procrastination. We were talking at the time about his plans for the fall semester when Ben offhandedly misspoke a word.

"I'm going back several days early irregardless . . ." he began.

"Wait, *irregardless*, is that a word?" he asked, followed by, "Is it *irregardless* or *regardless*?"

"Regardless," I offered, as Ben shook his head, visibly embarrassed and flustered, far out of proportion to an innocuously misspoken word.

"I *hate* when I do that," he sputtered. "When I was in high school, that never bothered me; I would just talk myself around what I wanted to say. But I can't do that now. I try to sound like an adult, and I just feel so stupid when I don't know the word or say it wrong."

After a few moments, Ben looked up from his embarrassment and said, "That's what those phone calls were about, the ones I didn't want to make. I was just so worried about saying something stupid, afraid they'd think, *This is just some kid!*"

Ben's experience—such an emotional hang-up over such an apparently trivial matter—is startlingly typical of the secret fears that transitioners have of being exposed as phonies and pretenders in the world of adults. When we encounter a struggling transitioner who is anxious in the face of an obvious developmental benchmark—leaving for college, getting ready to depart for military boot camp, or signing an apartment lease—their anxiety makes obvious sense to us, and to the transitioner him- or herself as well. Anxiety in these circumstances makes sense because it is easily connected with an impending life-changing event, an official upgrade in developmental status. And because it more or less makes sense to everyone involved, transitioners are more likely to accept support and encouragement, and adults are much more likely to offer it. But in cases like Zach's and

Ben's, where the anxiety and avoidance are triggered *not* by a life-changing benchmark but by a seemingly inconsequential administrative task, we are all—the transitioner included—left scratching our heads.

Anxiety such as Ben's is a natural consequence of the uncertainty and disorientation that often accompanies change. It's *developmental anxiety*, rather than a symptom of clinical disorder. Almost anyone who has ever started a new job or has received a promotion has felt the tensions that result when one is facing new expectations and responsibilities. The uncertainty of the new situation, together with the challenge of having to prove oneself, produce for many a kind of ambivalence, an admixture of excitement and apprehension about the impending transition.

For transitioners like Ben and Zach, the promotion in question is on a different scale than that of an adult taking on new responsibilities or a new job. It's on a different scale because it involves, quite literally, a transformation of developmental status. The "promotion" to emerging adulthood opens up a new horizon of expectations and benchmarks, alters the experience of self and identity, and requires letting go of the safe and predictable habit patterns of childhood and adolescence. In this light, it should not be surprising to us when we encounter evidence of an intense underlying ambivalence regarding these simple but deeply significant tasks.

It is because this anxiety is so fundamental and pervasive that it is hard to pin down rationally, and why so often it is expressed in "irrational" aversions to the small symbolic administrative tasks of adult responsibility. The necessary phone call, the overdrawn checking account, the unpaid parking ticket—none of these by themselves amount to much except for the fact that *adolescents don't generally attend to these things, whereas adults do.* And that's precisely the issue. Beneath this ambivalence and anxiety lie two deeply rooted and intimately intertwined questions.

Question 1. Am I Capable?

The first question a struggling emergent adult asks him- or herself is "Can I do this? Am I capable? Do I know what I'm doing? Or am I in over my head?" These are all versions of the same question—what I label the *competence question.* We tend to think of competence as an objective quality, judged on the basis of a person's measurable and observable capabilities and accomplishments. Does he know how to write that essay? Does she have the skills to pick up the phone and make that call? Of course the answer is yes.

But I am interested in competence as a *subjective* experience, which is something else entirely, and often disconnected from an individual's "objective" capabilities. The young child who stands frozen on the end of the high diving board isn't so much *in*competent as he is *pre*-competent. He is consumed by his private world of uncertainty and fear, having not yet had the actual experience of mastering the leap into the water. Before the child takes that first leap, his *own* sense of competence, regardless of what his parents or swimming instructor judge to be the case, is still an open question.

This was the case for Ben, and for almost every transitioner who can't find the courage necessary to read the fine print on his parking ticket or contact the bank about his overdrafts or call the doctor's office to reschedule an appointment. Struggling transitioners are notoriously avoidant of these sorts of small administrative challenges, and the underlying reason almost always has to do with a deeper underlying anxiety about taking on the mantle of being a grown-up. Like Ben, these seemingly small challenges touch directly upon their fears of feeling overmatched, underprepared, ignorant, incompetent, stupid, and ashamed in the face of adult-world expectations. It wasn't the phone call itself that intimidated Ben; it was the expectation that he pass himself off as an adult. The task may indeed have been small, but the risk felt anything but.

This experience of self-doubt and uncertainty is not confined to young people knocking on the door of adulthood. Many card-carrying adults can readily identify with the anxiety that attends new experiences and unfamiliar circumstances. I recall several years ago when I was invited to teach a group of psychotherapists in Slovenia. I needed to visit a bank for some reason I can't quite recall, and when I entered the building, I found myself immediately disoriented. It didn't resemble any bank I had ever visited, and I was confused about which person to approach and where to transact my business. It felt instantaneously like a flashback experience to me—I was twenty years old again, stepping into the foreign territory of the adult world, and I felt small and stupid for not knowing the first thing about how to proceed. Thank God my wife was at my side, as she takes unfamiliarity in stride and gracefully decodes the novelty of almost any situation.

In my adult work life, I am much more self-assured. Like many reasonably seasoned professionals, I approach new challenges with an attitude of *comfortable uncertainty*: "I haven't done this before . . . but it seems within my capabilities . . . let's try and find out." But this comfort with challenge wasn't always the case. When I wrote my first book, some years ago, I *thought* I had something to say, but I also harbored deep insecurities, wondering whether I was just fooling myself. And years before that, when I took my first position as a twenty-seven-year-old newly minted PhD and people began addressing me as "Doctor," I was secretly terrified that I would be found out as a fraud—because, really, how much do most twenty-seven-year-olds know about the challenges and complexities of adulthood, parenting, and the real world?

Retracing my developmental steps further, when I began graduate school immediately after college, my sole objective was to avoid flunking out, and I lived on the edge of fear that I would not measure up to the high standards of my professors. And earlier yet, when as an undergraduate college student I decided to finally get serious about academics, to push myself and find out what I was really capable of (I had been a high school slacker, afraid to test my potential by exerting real effort), I experienced panic attacks and cascades of overwhelming anxiety.

We've all got our waiting-to-be-answered developmental questions, and mine, like so many transitioners, was always "What am I truly capable of?" My point is this: Whatever your own developmental questions, you have had, like me, opportunities to answer them, to test yourself, and to develop a realistic sense of confidence in your capabilities.

But transitioners, particularly struggling transitioners like Nick and Kyle and Bridie and Zach and Ben, are facing these important self- and life-defining questions *for the first time*, and that's the thing we adults so frequently forget when we are confronted with their seemingly irrational avoidance and neglect of everyday responsibilities. We forget the stakes. There was infinitely more on the line when, as an eighteen-year-old, I summoned the courage to throw myself into my college studies, to find out exactly what I was capable of—than when, for example, I decided to write this book.

Question 2. Will I Be Taken Seriously?

The second question underlying the transitioner's ambivalence—one closely related to the first—is "Will I be taken seriously? Will I be accepted, received, acknowledged as legitimate? Or will I be exposed as a pretender?" This is the *validation-shame question*. Shame is an emotion not well understood, but it's starting to be more deeply researched and recognized as a powerful force in our behavior from a very young age.

Shame is among the most social of all the human emotions. It has the hallmark, in the words of psychologist Jean-Marie Robine, that in the presence of other people, I experience myself as somehow *not what I am supposed to be*. It's a feeling that things are off with me and with the world around me, which is part of why it can be a particularly physical sensation (the hot face, the sweaty palms). Shame can be as mild as the embarrassment I feel when I forget the name of someone I have met before, or when I place my order at the deli counter and then discover that I have neglected to take a number and wait my turn. We all have such moments of mild shame occasionally, and we typically recover from them as soon as we leave the situation.

Yet shame can be much more serious and debilitating than this, as when experiencing oneself as deeply flawed or fundamentally inadequate in the face of real or imagined expectations of others. In contrast to mild shame, where I feel like I am *doing* something wrong, serious, toxic shame involves the feeling that I *am* wrong; as Robine says, "I'm not what I'm supposed to be." This sort of shame can be toxic, and it can severely impede one's everyday life and, in the case of young people, their progress into emerging adulthood.

Unraveling the DNA of the validation-shame question will help us make sense of young people like Zach and Ben, who retreat from interacting with the adult world. There are two essential ingredients underlying this question. The first is that the issue at hand is always something that *matters* to the individual. The father of modern shame research, Gershen Kaufman, concluded that we are vulnerable to shame only to the extent that we *care about* something. This may seem obvious, but it helps us to understand the opposite case—the experience among transitioners like Zach and Ben of purposively and actively *choosing to not care* about certain issues, as a defense against the possibility of shame.

The second essential aspect of the validation-shame question is that it is intrinsically social. In other words, you can't experience either validation or shame outside the context of your involvement with other people. Being received, validated, and taken seriously by other people perfectly describes the precarious situation for so many transitioners in their first tentative engagement with the adult world. They *want* to progress into different roles with new people, but the fear they will make a misstep in these unfamiliar environments (and the shame they feel when inevitably they do) can be immobilizing.

But of course a person's sense of self and identity is always and necessarily developed through interaction with the social world. Taking myself seriously requires a history of experiences in which I found *others* to take me seriously. My own professional self-concept includes elements of being a psychotherapist, a teacher, and a writer. These "concepts" didn't originate in my head. They emerged from a series of real-life interactions in which clients, students, and readers took me (more or less) seriously. The shame theorist Robert Lee has done the most to establish the connection between shame, self-esteem, and identity, brilliantly pointing out that self-confidence is nothing other than confidence that I will be received and validated by others. Lee goes on to say that the experience of *not* being received and validated by others is the essence of shame. As author and teacher Brené Brown emphasizes, shame doesn't simply result from my private experience of being flawed and imperfect. It results from the fact that my (inevitable) flaws and imperfections render me *vulnerable* in my interface with the social world.

The universal response to shame is to run and hide, to escape the exposure and humiliation of being revealed as inadequate. For *most* transitioners, the small behavioral forays into the territory of adulthood are at worst possibilities for mild embarrassment or awkwardness. But frequently enough, we encounter young people like Zach and Ben, for whom the simple task of making an "adult" phone call presents the danger of being revealed as a pretender and introduces the possibility of substantial shame and humiliation.

Beyond these small but significant vulnerabilities, I frequently encounter more profound instances of the same "Will I be taken seriously?" issue. One twenty-six-year-old client of mine, when asked why he had dropped out of college several years previous, in spite of the fact that he was doing well academically, told me the following heartrending story. When he was in high school and suffering the angst of being fifteen and discovering his inner emotional world, he began to read poetry as a way of mirroring his own emergent, private experience. He read Billy Collins when he was feeling good about life and Sylvia Plath when he wasn't. Poetry became important to him and a way of mapping and understanding his inner world. He kept a (very) private journal, in which he crafted his own original poems. Near the end of high school, he even found the courage to participate in an informal poetry slam in an English class.

Once in college, he entertained the aspiration of studying literature and perhaps becoming a real poet himself. Aspiring to become an artist of any sort is risky emotional business, to say the least, as the criteria for judging talent and success can be difficult to ascertain. To an extreme degree, the issue of whether you are in fact, an artist, comes down to the question of "Am I taken seriously?" by people who matter.

His first heroic excursion beyond the safe confines of his high school English class and his personal poetry journal came in a creative writing class, when he volunteered to read one of his poems aloud. My client couldn't recall his professor's exact words, but remembered that they were dismissive, and that his acute sense of humiliation and shame led him on a precipitous downhill slide that involved never returning to the class, followed several very depressed weeks later by dropping out of college altogether. He felt exposed as a fraud and a failure, and it took him several years to take himself seriously enough to return to university studies.

Just the opposite story was told to me a week ago by Henry, a twenty-six-year-old photographer, currently committed to establishing himself as a high-end artist and technician. I knew his background, because I had seen him in therapy twelve years previously as an anxious adolescent whose tendency was to avoid anything that involved the possibility of failure or embarrassment.

What I wanted to know now, twelve years later, was how Henry, previously risk-averse to the extreme, had found the courage necessary to take himself seriously as an aspiring artist—something I know from clinical experience involves considerable vulnerability. He told me one of the most moving stories I have heard in my decades as a psychotherapist. Here's his story.

High school and the first year of college had been difficult for Henry. He was mildly dyslexic, and managed adequate grades only with considerable effort. What he much preferred to the classroom and schoolwork was a camera and a day wandering the streets of the town where he lived. It was a hobby, an outlet that relieved the stress of the slog of formal academics. Once in college, he casually decided to take a photography class as an elective. But "casual" was a front. Henry had received a fair amount of positive feedback from friends and classmates for his photography. And when he perused published photography books in the library, he thought, *I can do better.* This was not anything he would say to anyone, and certainly not to his college photography professor, for fear of being dismissed and ridiculed for such a "grandiose" aspiration.

But his professor did in fact give Henry some encouraging feedback, and with that support, he changed his major to photography. But still he was one among many, and while he thought more highly of his own work than that of his classmates, he was not about to share this dangerous thought with anyone.

Then something happened, something that proved transformative. He was taking a class with a visiting professor who was internationally known and respected for her work and expertise. He described the following scenario (and by the way, sobbed deeply throughout the telling, as he had never shared this story before). He brought a print from the darkroom (he was recognized in the department for his technical competence), one that was to fulfill a requirement for the course, and showed it to the professor.

"That's wonderful," she said. "You're finished."

Henry looked at the print for quite a while, and then said,

"No, it's not quite right . . . I want to take it back to the lab and run it one more time."

"No need," she said. But Henry insisted.

At that point, the famous professor stopped and looked Henry in the eye, holding his gaze for a few moments, and said, "You want to be *great*, don't you" (a statement, not a question). He felt immediately taken aback, undressed, his facade of socially appropriate humility stripped away. His secret aspiration, his "grandiosity," was exposed, and he felt deeply embarrassed, because he did indeed want to be great, though he had barely admitted as much to himself, let alone anyone else.

But then the professor shifted her attention back to the print, looking at it for quite a long time, and then began to nod her head slowly. "You're right," she said, "it's good, not great . . . but it's *close* . . . Take it back to the lab."

And in that moment, Henry had that priceless experience of not only being taken seriously, but of being granted permission to take himself—with all his aspirations, and especially his desire to become a great photographer—seriously as well.

Parents should know:

- These two questions—*Am I capable?* and *Will I be taken seriously?*—are implicitly present in most experiments in emerging adult behavior.
- If you've got a transitioner who is mysteriously resisting apparently inconsequential or innocuous tasks, it's a good bet that he or she is feeling threatened by the seemingly

adult nature of the task, its unfamiliarity, and the perceived danger of embarrassment or humiliation. I recently sat with a father and his twenty-two-year-old son, monitoring their argument over whether the son needed a car in order to get back and forth to work. The son was adamant that a car was essential for working, whereas the father pointed out that they lived on a bus route that went directly into the business center of town. They went round and round, and I found myself initially perplexed by the intensity of the young man's insistence. Finally I excused the father from my office so that I could speak with his son alone.

Once he was gone, I turned to the young man, smiled a little mischievously, and queried: "You don't know how to take a bus, do you?" He looked surprised, stuttering, "Uh . . . uh . . ." I continued: "Do you pay when you get on? Or when you get off?" Not surprising, he had no idea and found it quite embarrassing to admit this. It's sad that he would feel this way but also not unusual, given that the average transitioner knows precious little about how the world actually works.

- Find some way of walking them through the task. With this young man, I counseled that he and his father go into town the following Saturday morning for breakfast—taking the bus together back and forth—which they did. By lunch-time, he had mastered public transportation.

- For the time being, the most supportive thing we can do as parents and professionals is to see through the avoidance to the anxiety and uncertainty that lie beneath. Remind yourself that it's not "just" a phone call; your transitioner knows how to make a phone call. What he doesn't know how to do—and may need your support and guidance to learn—is how to make a phone call *as an adult*.

Chapter 5

Skill 2
Becoming Relational

Emerging Adults Must Retool Their Relationships and Find New Sources of Support

Remember Bridie, from chapter 2? Bridie was the young girl who stormed out of her parents' home and went to live with her older sister shortly after high school graduation. Her plan was to grow up overnight, by virtue of cutting off all ties with mom and dad. I met her after her experiment in independence had fallen apart and an acute depressive collapse had brought her home. As I described earlier, my therapy work with Bridie and her parents resembled a crash course in adolescence, as I shepherded them through the evolving parent-child relationship changes of the teen years.

But there was more to Bridie's story than her need to revisit the curriculum of adolescence with her parents. Their protracted state of conflict rendered that relationship temporarily unhelpful, but what was equally striking was the absence of supportive relationships *anywhere* in her life, including with peers, older transitioners, or nonfamilial adults. Her older sister, with whom she lived, was absorbed in her medical school studies. Their relationship was more impersonal roommate than supportive sibling. Bridie basically had no one to talk to, no one who shared her confusion or anxiety, no one who had recently mastered the challenges she was facing, and no adult advisers to consult for encouragement or advice. Bridie, like many of the struggling transitioners I see in my practice, seemed to think that growing up is something you do on your own.

That's not how it works.

If we stop to consider all that must be accomplished in the transition from adolescence to emerging adulthood, we might well ask how *anyone* ever makes it. Absent the stabilizing life structure of high school and without the guidance and oversight of teachers and parents, what are the supports and anchors that keep young adults afloat and heading downstream amid the uncertainty and challenges of the post-adolescent transition?

The answer lies, often enough, in the kind and quality of relationships that transitioners form with others—peers, parents, and nonfamilial adults. The form that these relationships took during adolescence is often inadequate for what lies ahead, and must be upgraded and renegotiated as transitioners grow and mature. Relationships have to become more robust, more three-dimensional, more equal. They have to provide stimulation and support for the kinds of thinking and behavior that lead to adulthood.

Let's look at each of these relational domains—peers, real-world adults, and parents—and describe the developmental upgrades that support (and the failures that inhibit) the transition to emerging adulthood.

Peers: A New Kind of Friendship

Frequently the young person who has dropped out of school or who has failed to manage substance use and abuse or who just seems to be going nowhere is the one who has somehow failed to form genuine and supportive relationships in their post-high-school life. This isn't always obvious at first glance. Many struggling transitioners attain what *looks* like adequate social adjustment—they may have friends, be "popular," or become involved in a long-term romantic relationship. But beneath the surface, these social connections may lack the capacity to anchor and nourish the emerging adult self through the course of this transition. Worse yet, unhealthy relationships can drain the transitioning self of the vitality and courage necessary for the creative adjustments that true growth requires.

Travis was a typical case in point. He had chosen a college to attend on the basis of its proximity to his longtime high school girlfriend. For a year they traveled back and forth to each other's campuses on weekends and continued to spend time together during vacations. Then, in his sophomore year, the inevitable happened. His girlfriend gradually grew emotionally distant, eventually announcing that she had met a boy at school whom she wished to date. They went through an agonizing period of an "open" relationship, but she soon formally ended their romantic involvement entirely. Travis was devastated. He became depressed, he stopped going to class, he quit taking care of himself entirely. I first saw him in my office the day after his parents brought him home from school, and indeed he radiated an air of being lost and alone.

The great irony in Travis's case—and this is not at all unusual—was that his romantic relationship, for all its apparent intimacy, actually served to inhibit, even prevent, the sort of relationships that effectively support and anchor developing transitioners. He had no close friends other than his girlfriend, and his all-encompassing attachment to her prevented him from reaching out and forming new connections at college. When she broke up with him, he had no one to turn to—no friends who could really understand how devastated he felt, no one to sympathize and empathize, and no one to help distract him from painful emotions or to drag him back to class and urge him to attend to his studies.

He had put all his eggs into one basket, connection-wise. And when his relationship blew up, he felt hopelessly and utterly alone.

Allison was another college student whose capacity to function collapsed under the weight of clinical depression. On the surface, her story seemed diametrically opposed to Travis's. She was a superb athlete who had been recruited to play college soccer, and she displayed the sort of presence and interpersonal skill that earned her a co-captaincy of her squad. In high school she had likewise been a leader, attaining the sort of popularity that kept her social calendar full. Things unraveled quickly and surprisingly for Allison when she tore her anterior cruciate ligament on the playing field, requiring surgery and rehab and ending her athletic career for good. Soccer had been such a central part of her life that she felt lost without it. In the two months following her injury, her mood had spiraled inexorably downward, and she began to have anxiety episodes in which she felt strangely detached from the world around her.

When I first met Allison in my office, she was visibly uncomfortable and awkward, not at all resembling the confident young woman her parents had described.

"I don't do this," she announced hesitantly.

"Do what?" I asked.

"Get help," she answered. "People usually come to *me* for help, not the other way around." And indeed, Allison described for me a busy and connected social life, rich in every way but one: She had to be the "strong" one, and regarded any sort of turning to others for support as "weakness." Unlike Travis, who had put all his eggs in one basket, Allison had kept all her eggs to herself. But as different as they seemed before their respective lives blew up, when they walked through my door they looked very much alike.

The common thread for Allison and Travis is that neither had developed the sort of robust, supportive friendships that serve to anchor and stabilize transitioners in difficult times. He fell victim to a desperate, clinging dependency; she was felled by her self-limiting hyper-independence. Both had failed to establish a network of mature *interdependence* that could help them weather the storms of personal crisis.

In the adolescent world of high school, considerable energy is invested in establishing an identity in the social landscape of high school and peer culture. The focus is on developing social skills and a persona—what some social scientists have called *face*. In broad terms, social development in the adolescent years is about finding one's place in this landscape. It involves making friends, becoming part of social networks, and identifying roles and identities among peers. Developing an adolescent persona means developing one's trademark as a certain kind of person—athletic, funny, friendly, smart, rebellious, nice, confident, and so on. In the simplest terms, adolescent social development is about *fitting in* (or adjusting to the fact of *not* fitting in), and acquiring the social skills and social identity necessary to do so. The extraordinary role of social media in contemporary high school culture testifies to the central role of one's persona, or outward social identity, in this developmental process. This fact accounts for the familiar characterization of adolescents as exceedingly vulnerable to peer pressure and constrained by "the rule of cool."

By the end of the high school years, however, the underlying needs and organizing principles of friendships begin to change. For one thing, all this investment in social persona begins to grow tiresome, and transitioners often express a yearning for more genuine and fulfilling relationships. Many graduating seniors express relief at being nearly done with high school society and welcome the prospect of rebooting their social lives and identities in college.

A perfect example was Jason, an eighteen-year-old who consulted me the summer prior to leaving for college, concerning what he termed his "social anxiety disorder." This self-assessment would have come as a surprise to Jason's circle of high school friends had he shared it with them, because he came across among peers as affable and easygoing. He was, by his own description, popular, and he never lacked for people seeking his company for after-school and weekend hangouts.

So why did he come to see me? It turns out that Jason's adolescent social life had a hidden inner dimension that he was only now coming to articulate. He had been considerably overweight until recently, when a late growth spurt lengthened his frame.

"I got through by becoming the 'funny fat kid,'" he confided. "It was just sort of a role I figured out, and it worked." But now, as he matured, he had become acutely aware of this role for precisely what it was—a role. As I described earlier, he was moving beyond the stage of simply *immersing* himself in his relationships and was beginning to *reflect* upon them. As he matured, he found his familiar role to be increasingly restrictive and limiting for his interpersonal possibilities. For example, he pointed out, funny fat kids don't share their private worries and concerns; they don't engage in heart-to-heart talks—"serious conversations"—about life, the future, self-doubts, and so on. And—a factor that was increasingly frustrating for Jason—funny fat kids don't date, they don't have girlfriends, and they don't ever "hook up."

Jason is another of those kids I call "poets," speaking eloquently about what so many of their peers experience but rarely find words for. He had developed a social persona—an outer social self—that served well the high school mandate of fitting in, but that limited him in meeting his need for genuine and robust connections. Jason, like so many of his similarly constricted age-mates, couldn't wait to for high school to be over!

Throughout adolescence, a large measure of developmental support and direction is provided by the stabilizing influence of adult overseers (Mom, Dad, teachers, coaches). As young people transition from adolescence toward adulthood, however, more and more of this anchoring and orienting must be provided by the transitioner him- or herself. As a result, interpersonal peer relationships bear an ever-increasing load of the responsibility for support and stability. Friends matter more and more as transitioners get older, and that's as it should be. But as we saw with Travis and Allison, the failure to establish more robust, supportive three-dimensional relationships during the transitioning years creates real emotional vulnerability during episodes of stress or crisis.

Several years ago, I received an email from Travis's mother, telling me that he had successfully graduated from college and taken a promising full-time position in business. I had helped him through his period of depressive collapse while he was still a college student, and I was interested to learn how he had completed his transition to adulthood. So I asked if I could interview him for this book. The story he told was instructive. Around the time he stopped coming to therapy, he reconnected with his old high school clique. Travis and his friends essentially picked up where they had left off at around age sixteen, when Travis had abandoned the group for immersion in his ill-fated romantic relationship. The reconstituted group did a lot of good old-fashioned adolescent hanging out—watching movies, playing video games, telling fart jokes, and the like.

A year or so later, around the time he was reenrolling in college, the group began to dissolve, dying the natural death of most adolescent groups. In college, Travis formed several deeper friendships, bonding initially with these new pals around a shared history of prior emotional struggles and depression. These relationships have served as a stabilizing outrigger for Travis through his college years and beyond. At the time of my interview, Travis proudly announced that he is engaged to be married, with one of his college buddies lined up to be his best man.

Real-World Adults: The Art of Securing Support

When Kyle, our not-really-ready-for-college procrastinator from chapter 2, headed off to college, he was, sad to say, academically DOA. He had managed to successfully complete his high school curriculum with oodles of support from the adult world—his eagle-eyed private school teachers, his organizational coach, his calculus tutor, and of course, his parents. He had learned, quite unconsciously, to depend upon the surrounding adult world to proactively insinuate itself into his life whenever support was needed.

But the adult world around the transitioner is significantly different from that around the high school adolescent. The unwritten and unspoken ground rules have changed, as professors, coaches, physicians, therapists, and bosses orient themselves differently toward transitioners than they do toward adolescents. Consciously or unconsciously, they expect more in the way of self-direction and self-management. And accordingly, the adults in their lives feel less obligation and responsibility for shaping and guiding the transitioner's development. The college professor or workplace supervisor isn't going to call Mom and Dad if junior doesn't show up at the appointed time or if a bank account is overdrawn or if a speeding ticket goes unpaid.

This new paradigm requires the transitioner to take on more initiative in these relationships. If the mandate in high school was to be receptive to adult support and guidance, the mandate for transitioners is to learn how to actively pursue and procure that support from the adult world *for themselves*. This is a significant and important developmental shift, requiring the transitioner to take on the tasks of self-diagnosis and initiative when things aren't going well. But as we have seen with most of the young people introduced in these pages, reaching out and asking for support is not something most struggling transitioners have mastered.

Emerging adults themselves, as we learned earlier from Jeffrey Arnett's research, equate adult status with various expressions of independent functioning. Independence, common sense suggests, is the defining developmental task of emerging adulthood. This commonsense way of thinking about development, however, is flawed, based more upon assumptions and myth than facts. We assume that the opposite of dependence (needing others to take care of us) is rugged independence (needing only ourselves for support and caretaking).

This couldn't be further from the truth.

The psychologist Gordon Wheeler has carefully examined

this idea of independence, which he calls the paradigm of individualism, and demonstrated convincingly that it simply isn't supported by the facts. We have, Wheeler points out, an archetype in the American psyche of the fully developed person as one who stands alone, needing no one, depending only on themselves. Think of the John Rambos and Jeremiah Johnsons of American film, the Emersons and Thoreaus of literary fame, and the Pattons and MacArthurs of military history (and isn't it interesting that these cultural models are exclusively male!). We are inclined to view dependence of any sort as a weakness and to save our highest praise for the person who "goes it alone." "I don't need help from anyone; I'm my own man [or woman]" is an anthem of heroism in Western culture, and nowhere more so than in America.

This independent mind-set seeps into all of us, even (especially) young people. One of the most common traits of stalled and struggling transitioners is the self-destructive belief that accepting support and help is a sign of failure, inadequacy, and defeat. But the developmental truth is that hyper-dependence and hyper-independence *both* represent incomplete stages of development. If we look beyond cultural iconography for a moment and study instead genuinely happy and successful adults as models of maturity, we find lives that are rife with *inter*dependence. Interdependent relationships are what make adult relationships— marriages, business partnerships, lasting friendships—work.

So what's interdependence? For transitioners, it means forming relationships in which one both gives and takes. It means learning how to turn to friends for understanding and solace, it means learning how to seek counsel and guidance from those who are better informed, it means learning to accept one's insufficiencies as an unavoidable part of the equation, rather than as proof of inadequacy and failure. In what seems at first glance a paradox, we discover that the emergence of healthy and vibrant *self-reliance* for transitioners is very much contingent upon the availability of *support* in their interpersonal relationships. In fact, what we find is that the most critical developmental task for transitioners is to learn how to seek out, how to accept, and how to utilize support in a growth-enhancing fashion.

Allison the athlete, like so many of the struggling transitioners I have seen in therapy, viewed coming to see me as both a threat to her independence and a testimony to her weakness and failure. Neutralizing the awkwardness and shame of coming to therapy is frequently a crucial first phase of the process, but in Allison's case, it turned out to be the heart of the work. I asked her, during our second session, what she could envision herself doing after college.

"Maybe coaching," she conjectured.

"Do you know much about coaching?" I asked.

"Yeah, I think so," she replied. "I've been around a lot of coaches."

"So you know all about how to set up a program, how to find funding, how to deal with disgruntled parents?" I pressed.

"Well, not exactly." She thought for a moment. "I guess I'd talk to people who had done all that, get some pointers on the non-soccer parts of coaching."

"So you'd get yourself some coaching consultants," I continued.

"Yes, I guess so," she confirmed.

"And how much do you know about how dedicated athletes respond to serious injuries? How would you go about helping an athlete who became depressed and felt depersonalized on account of her injuries?"

Allison cocked her head and gave me a suspicious smile. "Where are you going with this?" she asked.

"Well, what does a smart person do when they don't know something that's important to know? They go find consultants. I don't know squat about soccer, but I know a lot about anxiety and depression, and about how disorienting it can be for athletes when part of their identity is suddenly stripped away from them." Allison looked at me steadily as I continued.

"Like it or not, that's stuff you need to learn about. You need a consultant. That's what I am. I'm a consultant who knows about stuff that you need to learn about. I'm not going to fix you. *You're* going to fix you. I can show you how. That's all; I'm just your consultant." When I framed our interaction that way, Allison was able to let down her guard and engage in meaningful conversation with me, setting aside her belief that accepting support would somehow make things worse.

In some ways, Allison reminded me of myself. I can still recall vividly my own experience as a neophyte psychologist, fresh out of graduate school. I had just joined the staff of a large community mental health center and was more than a little intimidated by the fact that people addressed me as "Doctor." I assumed, without even knowing it, that I was expected to know all the things I imagined a competent psychologist should know, which—of course—I did not. I regularly spent evenings poring through old textbooks, lecture notes, and journal articles, in a crazed pursuit to hide the shame of my (unavoidably) incomplete education. And like Allison, I felt that asking for support from colleagues would somehow invalidate my legitimacy—in their eyes and in my own. It was not until I swallowed my misguided pride, turned to colleagues for support, and learned to ask the "dumb" questions (that is to say, the real ones!) that I began to develop genuine competence.

When transitioners accept the value and necessity of procuring support from others with more experience, they are well on their way toward developing healthy, adult independence.

Parents: Horizontalizing the Relationship with Mom and Dad

The third area of relational retooling for transitioners, and in some ways the most important, is reshaping their relationships with their parents. In childhood and adolescence, there was a necessary asymmetry to the relationship, with the child's dependency and need complemented by the parents' benevolent authority and supervision. And while many transitioners retain some degree of financial dependence upon their parents, it is developmentally imperative that they achieve, psychologically and emotionally, equal footing with their parents. I call this developmental process *horizontalizing*, since it transforms the vertical, hierarchical relationship of parent and child during the period of childhood and adolescence into one more accurately described as adult to adult. Realistically, this developmental achievement takes ten to fifteen years, beginning in the throes of adolescence and culminating in the maturity of emerging adulthood. The transitioner's task is to take this process past its tipping point, where the relationship begins to feel, to both transitioner and parent alike, more adult than adolescent.

Sammy was a twenty-four-year-old example of what can happen when this specific developmental task is left untended. Sammy was a college graduate, very bright, and six months into a good job when he first came to me. Sammy didn't *look* like a struggling transitioner. He had no unpaid parking tickets, his checking account was not overdrawn, and he displayed no anxious avoidance of life's responsibilities. In fact, Sammy seemed well on his way toward adult self-reliance by all observable measures. And except for the fact that he found himself victim to "mysterious" recurring bouts of depression, which triggered episodic thoughts of suicide, I would have agreed.

My first impression was that Sammy's depression reflected a significant mismatch between his considerable intellectual talents and the skill set required for his job. At the advice of his father, Sammy had majored in business supply chain management, and upon graduation had taken a job with a national retail chain, scheduling and coordinating the shipping of goods to regional outlets. The work required attention to detail, and was, according to Sammy, repetitive and boring. His cognitive profile was much better suited to big-picture thinking and creative problem-solving. I have often had adult therapy clients whose malaise in life derived from just such a mismatch between their talents and their responsibilities.

"Why *this* job?" I inquired.

At first Sammy only shrugged. "The tight job market, I guess . . . this was the best offer I got." For the time being, this seemed a reasonable explanation. I began to wonder, however, several sessions later, when Sammy began telling me about his family.

His father, it turned out, was a highly successful executive and had advised Sammy that this position was an excellent portal to the sort of career that he himself enjoyed. Since Sammy didn't have any clear vision of his own future, he accepted his father's vision wholesale. This event, I soon learned, reflected the general tenor of Sammy's relationship with his parents. He was relentlessly deferential, regularly set aside his own agenda in service of theirs, and, not surprising, harbored a roiling but unexpressed resentment—a resentment that had congealed and was largely responsible for his "mysterious" depression.

The transitioner's task of horizontalizing his relationship with parents, when accomplished successfully, has two important components. First, it involves the transitioner's beginning to experience him- or herself more as a competent actor, as someone who can oversee his or her own growth and development. As someone who is capable of making important choices and getting them done. This gives a transitioner more power and a stronger sense of himself.

But at the same time, the transitioner begins to see his or her parents in a new light, too. He or she begins to see them as *real people*, just like him- or herself, albeit older, presumably wiser, and more established. The transitioner starts to transcend the adolescent relationship with his or her parents, when Mom and Dad were viewed as little more than an Uber service or a meal ticket. Rather than seeing our parents one-dimensionally (in terms of their impact upon our agenda), as we age we start to see them in more realistic terms—as ordinary human beings with their own feelings, values, vulnerabilities, and agendas. The relationship, in the words of developmental psychologist Robert Kegan, begins to display a quality of *mutuality*, with more reciprocal appreciation, more two-way give-and-take.

Kegan tells us that development, optimally, pushes beyond the me-first self-absorption classically associated with adolescence toward a new way of thinking. Impulsive self-interest gives way to a parent-child relationship of mutual regard and mutual respect. Kegan writes that in this transition to mutuality, the individual shifts from prioritizing "what will happen to me or my wants" to prioritizing "what will happen to my bond or connection or relationship." This is what every parent waits for—the moment when one's recent adolescent begins to feel like an adult, maybe even like a peer.

This process of learning to *see one's parents as people* ideally begins in the transitioner stage, but is not an all-at-once phenomenon. I vividly recollect sitting around our kitchen table one evening with family and friends, when we got to talking about "nativity stories"—sharing tales of drama and tribulation attending the births of our various children. Once the laughter settled and the older adults quieted down, my son spoke up, telling the story of the birth of his oldest son, Conor. He ended his tale with a kind and graciously exaggerated remark: "When Conor was born, every crazy thing my parents ever did . . . began to make sense to me." I'm certain that wasn't quite true, but the evolution of our mutuality was touching and meaningful to both my wife and me.

This developmental achievement—horizontalizing one's relationship with one's parents—has significant positive consequences for the transitioner. For one thing, it affirms and enhances the transitioner's new sense of *feeling like an adult*. For another, now beginning to see his or her parents as ordinary people, the transitioner begins to *develop a tolerance of parental disappointment and disapproval*, both real and imagined. This is not to say that parental disappointment becomes irrelevant; rather, it becomes *bearable*. This is an incredibly important dimension of beginning to think, feel, and behave like an independent adult.

For Sammy, on the other hand, the thought of his parents' (particularly his father's) disapproval and disappointment felt unbearable, and accordingly, he avoided it at every turn. In fact, Sammy was so attentive to what mattered to his parents that he barely knew what mattered to himself.

In therapy with me and in joint sessions with his parents, Sammy learned to identify and articulate his own vision of an adult career path, eventually quitting his job and applying to graduate school to study economics. His father had a somewhat dim view of economists, being more of an operations man himself. But he grew to understand and even support Sammy's decision, and once he saw how excited and committed his son was to this new path, he even offered limited financial support for this endeavor.

When I began my work with Sammy, he described his father one-dimensionally as an uncompromising bully—someone "you could never talk to," someone who would become angry if anyone disagreed with him. My interpretation was that Sammy still saw his father through the eyes of a child. As Sammy learned in therapy to trust his own judgment, he increasingly came to see his father as an ordinary flawed human being. His father was indeed somewhat narrow-minded and overly confident in his own judgments—but he was also a man who deeply loved his son and was doing what he thought would help Sammy to achieve a happy, productive adulthood. I imagine that Sammy will always have to contend with his father's hardheaded nature. But because of his work in horizontalizing the relationship, he has become capable of doing so with the status of an adult.

Why is it so difficult for so many families with struggling transitioners to change the rules of engagement that have characterized their relationships? Why do they struggle to transform the parent-adolescent relationship into one that more closely resembles adult to adult? If you ask struggling transitioners (which I have done hundreds of times), they will tell you it's because their parents continue to treat them like adolescents. On the other hand, if you ask their parents, they will explain that the problem is just the opposite, maintaining that their transitioner continues to behave like an adolescent. Each perceives and believes that the other is calling the tune.

The fact is that *both* sides are right. In many respects, struggling transitioners continue to act like adolescents, and in many ways their parents continue to think and behave like the parents of teenagers. Each sees the other as the cause, but in truth both parent and transitioner are trapped in a dance that each side perpetuates. To find a way out of this interlocking puzzle, we have to understand the concept of *relational paradigms*. A relational paradigm refers to the underlying invisible, unspoken, even unconscious ground rules that organize and regulate most human relationships.

If you are engaged in a simple conversation with another person, you will behave differently depending on whether the person is your boss or your spouse or your psychiatrist or your banker. There are underlying ground rules about what's relevant, what's appropriate (and inappropriate), what's possible, and so on. Not surprising, these paradigms are often resistant to change. If your coworker becomes your boss or your boss becomes your tennis partner, you will likely find the underlying ground rules and protocols of the relationship resistant to change.

The same is true in parent-child relationships. We'll look at this idea more closely in chapter 8, but for now it's enough to know that your relationship with your struggling transitioner is strongly influenced, *on both sides*, by an underlying set of expectations, assumptions, and ground rules resistant to change. Old habits die hard, but die they must if your transitioner is going to find his or her way to adulthood. I'm raising this point to help you appreciate that there are inherent inertial forces (for which no individual is to blame!) that can escalate the developmental task of horizontalizing into a *challenge*—or even a *crisis*.

A close friend of mine described the transformation of his relationship with his daughter between the closing months of high school and the time of her leaving for college, a matter of about four months. She was an excellent student, and throughout high school had maintained an open and warm relationship with both parents. They were like friends, he confided, and as parents they had been spared all the usual friction and jostling of most parent–teen relationships. This was true until the second half of her senior year of high school.

It was, he said, as if she became an adolescent overnight. Curfews, previously a formality, now became an issue of contentious negotiation and were regularly stretched and broken. She became decidedly less open and more deceptive, as arguments, groundings, and resentment (on both sides) became the order of the day. "We'd been spoiled," he admitted, "and when our relationship with our adolescent daughter became 'normal,' I think we were all thrown for a loop."

Around the time of graduation, sometime in late May, he had what he called "a brilliant and crazy idea." He sat his daughter down at the family breakfast table and confessed how tired he and her mother were of all the recent tension and conflict. He offered the following proposal: "You're going away in a little over three months," he began. "How about we fast-forward the calendar and all of us pretend it's September already? We'll remove your curfew; we won't ask you where you're going when you go out. All we want in return is your commitment to conduct yourself in a manner that is both responsible and respectful. We'll treat you like an adult; you agree to conduct yourself like one. Let's try this for a month and see how it goes."

Needless to say, she accepted the offer in a flash, and they were off to the races. Except *races* turned out to be the wrong word. The situation was more like a demolition derby, from my friend's description. For the next four weeks, they saw little of their daughter, lost more sleep than they cared to admit, and felt as though they had spawned a party-girl monster rather than a responsible emerging adult. "Somehow we hung on," he related, "but it was very hard on us, particularly her mother." They kept waiting for the tide to turn, for a grown-up to emerge, but by the end of the month it was apparent that this was not about to happen.

One month later, both parents sat their daughter down and asked her, "How do you think this has worked out so far?"

"She didn't say a word," my friend reported. "She just looked down at her lap, clearly embarrassed, and remained silent." So he informed his daughter, in a calm, matter-of-fact manner, that her curfew was back in effect and all former house rules were reinstated. The truly interesting thing was that for the next month, his daughter played by these rules more or less willingly, and though not displaying the warmest of dispositions, conducted herself for the most part as a civil family member. She clearly knew that she had blown it and had accepted the reinstated house rules as a reasonable consequence of her behavior.

This in itself was an unmistakable sign of emerging maturity.

A few weeks later, my friend returned to the breakfast table with his daughter and asked her if she would like to have another go at living together under "adult rules." She accepted, of course, but this time the outcome was different as night from day. She kept reasonable hours, was thoughtful in letting her parents know what she was up to, and took pains to allay their inevitable worry if she was out late. In other words, she displayed the mutuality that Kegan describes as the hallmark of the paradigm shift from adolescence to emerging adulthood. She spent time at home and hung out with them from time to time, becoming engaged, conversational, participatory, and—above all—adult.

"It wasn't the same as before, earlier in high school, when she was compliant and gave us no trouble," my friend said. She was a "good kid" then, but now she was something different. She had transformed into a thoughtful, self-regulating young adult.

Please note that my friend always adds a caution when he tells this story: "Don't try this at home, folks." Nor do I offer this story as parenting advice but instead as a sort of time-elapse movie of the way that parent-child relationships evolve. Indeed, it's unmistakable when a transitioner passes through that tipping point and the relationship becomes truly more horizontal than vertical.

Parents should know:

- Your role in the life of your transitioner needs to begin to shift—from that of a *supervisor* who runs the show to a sort of *consultant* who's available as needed. This is called horizontalizing your relationship. Supervisors offer advice and instruction on their own initiative, when *they* think it's needed. Consultants offer advice when their "client" takes initiative and invites them to do so. If you have advice that might be beneficial to your transitioner, try to wrangle an invitation: "I know a lot about job searches . . . let me know if I can help you in any way." If your transitioner isn't open to your input, try arranging a consult with a non-threatening adult: "Your uncle Jack knows a lot about real estate; why not ask him to take a look at your lease?" You're still trying to help, but more in the fashion that one adult helps another, rather than the way a parent helps a child.
- In place of the organizing and stabilizing structure of the nuclear family, the transitioner needs to find substantial supportive relationships outside the family. These are of two primary types: relationships within his or her cohort of fellow transitioners, and relationships with older and more experienced representatives of the wider adult world. Again, parents can offer guidance and advice at times, but

the job of most parents at this stage is to do *less* for your child, not more.

- The critical developmental task for the transitioner, the task specific to this stage of life, is that of *supplying the initiative* for the formation of these relationships.

Chapter 6

Skill 3
Becoming Relevant

*Emerging Adults Must
Find a Sense of Direction*

On a recent vacation, I found myself midevening in one of those Instagram-perfect settings—sitting around a fire pit on a beach, sipping a beverage, making new friends. I struck up a conversation with a twenty-two-year-old and his girlfriend, listening to them talk about their current musical educational programs—hers, performance; his, production. At one point, he pulled out his phone and cued up a music video he had produced of her singing. I was expecting a YouTube, in-my-bedroom moment, but what he played was—at least to my uneducated eye—a polished, high-end, riveting video of a talented entertainer. And while I don't have the best ear for music production, I do have a good eye for people, particularly young people. I was captivated by their energy and enthusiasm as they talked about their interests and projects, and the self-possession with which they did. No bluster or braggadocio, just interest and energy and commitment. I couldn't help but smile, thinking, *I don't know where these kids are going . . . but I know they're going somewhere.*

These two aren't, I hardly need say, the young people who typically show up in my office.

In the previous two chapters, we looked at the developmental tasks of assuming ownership for administrative responsibilities and self-management, facing down the potential humiliation of being found out as an adult "pretender," forming interpersonal connections capable of supporting exploration and growth, and renegotiating new terms in one's relationship with parents. These are the achievements that enable transitioners to begin thinking, feeling, and behaving like grown-ups. When these accomplishments come together, they generate an integrated quality of personality that is deeper and more comprehensive than these component skills in isolation—a difference that is difficult to define, yet whose presence or absence we sense almost immediately. That something—what I sensed so clearly in those two young people I met on the beach—is a *sense of direction.*

Taking Ownership of the Future

A sense of direction is defined as acceptance and ownership of a personal future that *aims toward* adulthood. For young people, having a sense of direction is *not* the same as knowing what you want to do in life, having a career goal, or having a vision of success and satisfaction. In fact, as we saw with Kyle in chapter 3, the pressure that many transitioners feel to know their eventual adult careers can be utterly paralyzing, impeding rather than fostering an emergent sense of direction. When researchers identified adults in their forties and fifties who reported a high degree of satisfaction in their work lives and then took histories to determine the age at which these individuals found their occupational niches, the center of the bell curve for their discoveries was between ages twenty-eight and thirty-two. Occasionally people will know their life's work early in their development (my wife knew she wanted to be a teacher from about age twelve), but this is the exception, not the rule.

A sense of direction, in contrast to crystallized career goals, is more of an attitude or an orientation, a posture of faith and hopefulness toward the future. A sense of direction implies that the transitioner experiences him- or herself on a path leading toward the beckoning horizon of adulthood, and that adulthood—however vague and unspecified, however intimidating and confusing—is imagined to be essentially hospitable territory. The transitioner who has established a sense of direction exhibits an outlook that the philosopher Gabriel Marcel characterized as *existential hope*. Marcel formulated his theory of existential hope while a prisoner of war during World War I, when he sought to determine what enabled some prisoners to hang on in the face of grim prospects and great uncertainty, whereas others could not. Hope, according to Marcel, is very different from the goal-oriented motivation that we tend to associate with adult purposefulness (which Marcel called *desire*). Hope is more open-ended, and involves, paradoxically, a sort of "active waiting" for an outcome that is uncertain.

This hopefulness in the face of uncertainty is what creates a sense of direction, giving transitioners the courage to take ownership and responsibility for their ongoing and future development. For the transitioner who has accomplished this developmental task, the future is like more of a personal franchise, no longer "owned and operated" by adult management.

Conversely, when we encounter transitioners who have not accepted ownership of their future and lack this sense of direction, we frequently find people absorbed in the present tense of their lives, blocking out and avoiding any serious reflection or conversation about where their life is heading.

When a sense of direction is missing, we often encounter despair. In contemporary Western society, we probably encounter this sort of despair most regularly among young people from severely impoverished backgrounds—for example, in the "I don't expect to live past twenty-five" outlook of urban gang society or the desolate hopelessness of communities devastated by opioid addiction. But we also encounter it in the middle class among high school, college, and workforce dropouts, those living in their parents' basements, wasting away their futureless time with numbing chemicals and pointless diversions. In Marcel's insightful description, "despair is in a certain sense the consciousness of time as closed or, more exactly still, of time as a prison." In contrast, the transitioner with a sense of existential hope experiences time as open and beckoning, and conveys an underlying attitude of *looking forward* to his or her future.

This is not to say that those without direction don't have *desires*, in Marcel's sense. I am reminded of Annie, a twenty-three-year-old college dropout who filled her days with a single-minded devotion to her heroin addiction, and Robert, who filled his daylight hours with a dedicated study of poker strategy and nights online applying his knowledge in the pursuit of . . . what? He wasn't sure. Money, he guessed.

The surest sign that a transitioner has acquired a sense of direction is a commitment to activities that help to prepare one for adulthood. This can be going to school, learning a trade, joining the workforce, developing marketable knowledge and skills, signing up with the armed forces—any of which can provide a transitioner with a sense of direction and a nascent sense of relevance to the adult world.

This sense of direction toward the future is the *élan vital* that organizes, energizes, and constructively mobilizes a young person, creating a distinct impression of momentum, possibility, and purpose. Meeting and engaging a transitioner, we can feel his or her sense of purpose when it is present, just as we can sense the energy vacuum and inertia when it is not. It is what gives us that unmistakable impression that this person is eventually *going somewhere,* or alternatively, that sinking feeling in the pit of our stomach when we sense that they are stalled, stuck, and scared.

No Direction Known

That sinking feeling in the pit of the stomach is a perfect description of what I felt when I met twenty-two-year-old Andrew.

He came at the insistence of his father, who had grown increasingly concerned about Andrew's deepening depression. Andrew was a poster child for the going-nowhere twentysomething living at his father's house ("I don't live *with* him; I live *at his house*," Andrew emphasized), and working part time at a computer superstore. He was exceptionally bright, though only a so-so high school student due to his uninterest and lack of effort. Nevertheless, he had aced his SATs and gone off to college on a partial academic scholarship. He did well in computer science classes (computers were his thing), but otherwise found school irrelevant and boring. Two semesters of not going to class, staying up all night, smoking pot, and losing himself in a variety of pointless diversions resulted in Andrew's losing his scholarship and being suspended for academic reasons.

Once home and reinstalled in his old bedroom, Andrew continued to be aimless. Required by his father to work, he found the computer store job, where he connected with a small coterie of associates who shared his dismal worldview and with whom he shared a predilection for an online role-playing game (RPG) called World of Warcraft (WOW).

When Andrew and I met, he had been out of college for two and a half years and was near the bottom of a gradual but relentless downward spiral. His self-diagnosis was just that life was overwhelmingly boring, though he conceded that there was increasing evidence for his father's contention that he was clinically depressed. He had acceded, about a year earlier, to his father's request that he try antidepressant medication—

sometimes remembering to take the pills, sometimes not. He didn't think they helped.

In person, in one-to-one conversation, Andrew revealed the aimlessness and emptiness of his life. He was intellectually vacuous, vague in his verbalizations, and generally not interested in me or in what I might have to offer. He didn't "see the point," he'd say. Therapy was likely to be "just a bunch of bullshit, pretty much like everything else," he said whenever I pressed him about his reluctance to invest interest and energy in our time together.

Andrew showed many of the signs of clinical depression, and these were undoubtedly amplified and aggravated by his continued substance use. He failed to take care of himself, his attention and concentration were limited, and his motivational reservoir was pretty much empty. He had minimal enthusiasm for his work and no apparent interest in preparing for the future. He was, by his own description, a "night person" who split his waking hours between obligatory part-time shifts at work and hours holed up in his room playing WOW on his computer. He slept late, smoked heavily, and ate only what was readily available— fast food or his father's leftovers.

What does it mean, though, to say that Andrew was clinically depressed? We live in an era that regards depression as primarily a biological phenomenon—neurotransmitters out of balance, serotonin in retreat, dopamine in short supply. The problem, modern psychiatry tells us, was with Andrew's brain. And Andrew's plight was by no means unique. Young people are diagnosed today with depression and prescribed medication at alarming rates.

But when we are confronted with a living, breathing depressed transitioner like Andrew—someone who is turning his back on life at the entry point to adulthood—it's not enough to ascribe his situation to a faulty brain or a chemical imbalance. We must ask, *What does all this mean?* How did Andrew get so far off course in the first place? What is it about Andrew's life story that triggered this downward spiral and keeps him trapped in its vortex? What distinguishes Andrew from clinically depressed young people who *do* effectively manage their depressions, maintaining their developmental momentum in spite of their diagnoses?

If you've got an Andrew in your life—your son or daughter, your nephew or niece, your student or your client—you need to look beyond the presumed biological undertow and make sense of the ennui that he or she has defaulted to in lieu of a *sense of direction.*

Andrew's recounting of his family's story provided context. The younger of two boys, he felt closer to his older brother than to either of his parents. He described his parents (paraphrasing Thoreau) as "enslaved to their work, living lives of quiet desperation." Both were professionals: his mother an attorney and his father a university professor. In Andrew's assessment, neither their work nor their marriage gave either any joy. His relationship with his brother was his only oasis of connection and satisfaction.

As Andrew entered the tenth grade, his brother left for college. Eight months later, his mother abruptly and unexpectedly left his father. In the wake of these departures, his dour and disengaged father immersed himself only more deeply in his work. During his final two years of high school, Andrew essentially lived alone, his family having disintegrated around him. Andrew didn't become depressed initially, at least in the sense of exhibiting clinical symptoms. But there was a telltale emptiness in the high school history he recounted. He didn't care much for school, but did enough to get by. He wasn't socially isolated, but his involvements sounded superficial and activity-based, rather than providing any deeper connection and anchoring.

Finding the "Campfire in the Cave"

Andrew's depression was an expression of an existential meaninglessness, an absence of hope that grew over time. Andrew's future was not a beckoning profusion of possibilities, but an empty, barren void.

The challenge with depressed transitioners is to find a way to reach through their protective wall of detachment and lack of interest to discover what I call the "campfire in the cave." Engaging a young client like Andrew is like wandering into a dark cave, where you can't get a grip on anything, can't find purchase, and can't see the layout or the logic. But I've learned from experience that somewhere in the far reaches of the cave, there is always a sort of "campfire" burning. There is some ember of interest, some hoarded treasure of energy and investment, purposely hidden from the critical purview of the adult world. In Andrew's case, this was WOW, to which he withdrew as he avoided the demands of the "real world."

WOW is exactly what its title implies—a world. A player creates a character (usually something otherworldly, like a dwarf or wizard or troll), and endows that character with a personality, defined by its proclivities and powers (to fight, heal, cast spells, etc.). As that character, the player enters a fantasy world complete in every way—geography, politics, institutions (such as banks), and affiliations (guilds of like-minded compatriots). As a citizen of that world, the player is forced to make his or her own way, via quests, pursuing objectives, and acquiring wealth. Over time, players acquire the invaluable meta-commodity of *experience*, which is the gaming-world equivalent of status, power, and maturity.

For Andrew, WOW was the only activity that really mattered. He was actively invested in his guild, which amounted to a virtual community with its own website, chat boards, meetings, rules, and regulations. He held a position of importance in his guild: organizing quests, allocating spoils of conquests to guild members, updating the website, and so on. What this did for Andrew, of course, was supply his life with a *virtual* sense of direction and relevance. False direction and imaginary relevance, we might say, but direction and relevance nonetheless—precisely what was missing from his real life, outside the cave.

WOW provided Andrew with a *bubble world*, a world apart

from real life. In this bubble world, Andrew built a substitute life structure, with a network of involvements, commitments, objectives, obligations, and relationships. All of this served to organize and anchor his substitute sense of himself as competent, valuable, and relevant.

Holding Environments Provide a Bridge

Bubble worlds are similar to what psychologists call *holding environments*—life settings that provide supportive relationships and meaningful challenges. These holding environments foster, over time, growth and development. Holding environments include such settings as full-time jobs, structured gap-year experiences, or summers of backpacking the Appalachian Trail. They promote learning in their own right, but more important, they foster a sense of direction toward an adult future. The same could be said of volunteer work, treatment programs, therapeutic schools, and adventure learning programs (such as Outward Bound and the National Outdoor Leadership School). Colleges, graduate schools, postgraduate service programs, and tours of duty in the armed services also serve the same purpose. These are holding environments on a large scale, playing a crucial role in generating and supporting a sense of direction.

Mentors in holding environments are the purveyors of a wealth of helpful wisdom. When I worked with Kyle regarding his mistaken belief that he had to know his destination before beginning this journey, he asked how I had gotten my start.

"Well," I replied, "I knew that college was important, but I had no idea where it might lead. I wasn't a very disciplined student when I began, and just figured: *If I have to do this, I might as well choose something I find interesting.* For me that turned out to be psychology, but I had no designs on becoming a psychologist until much later."

Mentoring can occur in the form of psychotherapy, but it occurs with all manner of holding environment citizens—professors, bosses, older peers, age-mates, and so on. A holding environment, as Robert Kegan puts it in *In over Our Heads,* "provides both welcoming acknowledgment to exactly who the person is right now as he or she is, and fosters the person's psychological evolution. As such, a holding environment is a tricky transitional culture, an evolutionary bridge, a context for crossing over." The environment has a "mind" of its own, shaping the transitioner's days, weeks, months, objectives, and relationships. It provides a temporary life structure, enabling transitioners to answer the important questions of this developmental stage: "What do I like?" and "What am I good at?"

However vague or nonexistent a transitioner's sense of direction may be when he or she enters a holding environment, it will likely take shape by the time he or she leaves it. Remember Nick from chapter 1, who lived in his parents' basement and worked part time? His most important and "meaningful" activity was his nightly session at his neighborhood tavern. The tavern was Nick's substitute for a holding environment. We saw something similar with Andrew, in his intense immersion in WOW. I'm not suggesting that there's nothing to be learned at a neighborhood

tavern or in online gaming communities, but for Nick and Andrew these involvements served as *bubble worlds* rather than genuine holding environments.

A bubble world fulfills *some* of the emotional requirements of
a holding environment—organizing behavior, creating a network of relationships, and perhaps generating a sense of belonging and purpose. In this sense, they can serve the purpose of
anchoring and stabilizing a life structure. Most adults with
deeply fulfilling lives inhabit a bubble world or two. I have a dear
friend and golf companion, a successful and respected architect
who studies poker strategies and enters local poker tourna-
ments. He claims to win more often than he loses. Several other
of my golf cronies are deeply involved in the sport of curling
every winter. And if you hadn't figured this out yet, the wonderful, mysterious, infinitely fascinating game of golf is one of my
primary bubble worlds. And of course there are thousands of
other such delightful obsessions that contribute to the richness
of adult life—everything from playing bridge to bird-watching
to geocaching to gardening.

Yet bubble worlds for struggling transitioners are an entirely
different matter, because however much they mesmerize for the
moment, they drain one's energy and obstruct the development
of a sense of direction. There are two critical failures inherent in
bubble worlds for transitioners. First, they don't establish a sense
of movement and direction toward the adult world; instead,
they're like merry-go-rounds—apparent movement that leads
nowhere. When you get off, you're pretty much at the same place

where you got on. Second, bubble worlds are fragile and can burst at any time. Comrades move on, money runs out, the activity becomes boring, and so on. It creates a temporary sense of security, but no path to the future.

Modeling the "Real World" Offers a Path

In addition to holding environments, a second factor influencing a transitioner's sense of direction (or lack thereof) is the *modeling* of adulthood that the transitioner experienced earlier in life. As I've said previously, every child, for the most part unconsciously, develops a "theory" of what adulthood is like. This theory is inferred from living with adults, watching them go about their daily lives, and drawing implicit conclusions concerning what it all means—and what it would be like to be one of them. Do adults have fun? Do they seem to worry all the time? Do they seem to like what they do, even if what they do in the eyes of a child is rather mysterious? Do they have friends? Do they play? Do they seem to love each other?

Once, as a small child, I sat on the top step of the stairs, up way past my bedtime, while my parents entertained a group of friends downstairs. None of us children could get to sleep, because the house was filled with laughter rolling up the stairs, sometimes in convulsive fits. Two thoughts occurred to me at the time. First, *What do these adults find so funny?* And second, *Adulthood must really be a lot of fun!* I won't suggest that I didn't have my full share of challenges while growing up, but even when the path seemed obscure and steep, that childhood image of adulthood as hospitable territory kept me moving forward.

It is well established that children whose parents are un-happily married approach intimate relationships in adulthood with greater caution than others. Yet even beyond their parents' marriage, children are attuned to and take in a broad range of adult behavior. The child's developing psyche absorbs and di-gests parental attitudes toward education, politics, wealth, social justice—the list is virtually infinite. Included in this adult pal-ette of dispositions are parental attitudes toward the fundamen-tal roles of being an adult, such as earning a living, fulfilling one's responsibilities, and raising children. Children learn by observing their parents' relationships to their adult roles; this influences children's beliefs as to whether achieving adult status is likely to be a ripe or rotten plum.

As is true of so many products of childhood observation and inference, these intuitive observations and theories lie dormant throughout childhood, emerging only as a child approaches an age when they become relevant. And when these long-held (and often unsophisticated and childlike) theories do emerge psycho-logically, they typically arrive as *feelings*, rather than as thoughts or conscious beliefs. As feelings, they can exert a powerful va-lence of attraction or repulsion toward the prospect of becoming an adult oneself. Andrew was a perfect case in point. He saw his own parents living lives of quiet desperation, and with a des-peration all his own, he avoided joining their ranks at almost any cost.

Mentoring Shows a Way Forward

The third crucial factor in the emergence and reinforcement of a sense of direction involves what might best be described as mentoring. Mentoring means having contact with an adult who leaves the transitioner feeling known and valued—in short, *relevant* in the world of adulthood. That adult may be an employer, a teacher or professor, a relative (usually not one's parents, as a mentor represents the wider adult world beyond the family), or, as is often the case in my work, a therapist. The contact may be brief or prolonged, and it may involve many adults or one in particular. The essential feature is a contact that stimulates the transitioner's experience of relevance to the adult world and generates hope that he or she might find a place in that world.

Much of what I do in my psychotherapeutic work with struggling transitioners is to find the "campfire in the cave," something that can provide the kind of interest and validation that generates an experience of potential direction and relevance. I attempted this with Andrew, but I couldn't find a way to induce him to become interested in our relationship or in what I might have to offer. My therapy sessions with him reflected the stagnant energy of his life in general, going nowhere. He came only because his father required therapy as a condition for the used car that he provided.

But then something unforeseen happened. A friend of mine asked for advice concerning his sixteen-year-old son, who had recently become engrossed in a computer game called . . . World of Warcraft! He wondered if I knew anything about it. "Not really," I answered. "But I know someone who does."

Trusting my clinical intuition that something might be gained for all parties, I brokered a coffee-shop meeting between my friend and Andrew, selling Andrew on the idea that someone needed his expertise and that this would be his first gig as a real-world consultant. He was anxious at the prospect (though he would hardly admit it), as he had never considered that something he knew would be found valuable by the adult world. The meeting took place, with Andrew giving my friend a two-hour tutorial on the ins and outs of WOW, after which my friend peeled off two crisp twenty-dollar bills for Andrew's time. Both seemed satisfied with their takeaways.

But there's more to the story. My friend owns a home-remodeling and maintenance company, which has given him a great deal of experience in hiring and managing twentysomethings for work crews. This has made him a skilled communicator with young people like Andrew. In fact, their conversation turned out to be far more therapeutic than anything I could have engineered. For example, Andrew warned my friend that WOW can become addictive—something he had steadfastly refused to concede in sessions with me. He went so far as to suggest guidelines my friend might consider for limiting his son's interest and playing time.

The Andrew that my friend spent two hours with in the coffee shop was an Andrew I had never met. My friend described him as knowledgeable, forthcoming, smart, and strategic. He observed an aura of energy and investment that I had not encountered. In other words, the Andrew my friend met was *not* the clinically depressed cynic who showed up at my office each week, but a relatively well-put-together, animated, clear-thinking young man—a person who seemed to be going somewhere, rather than someone "stalled, stuck, and scared," the impression I mentioned at the beginning of this chapter.

When the meeting ended, my friend said goodbye to Andrew with a perfunctory "Hey, if you're ever looking for work, give me a call; I hire a lot of kids your age." Andrew mentioned that to me in our next session, and several months later, as he was complaining about the fact that his work hours were being reduced, I repeated it back to him. It took a while, but he did make the call—and soon he was working thirty hours a week cleaning gutters and taping windows for painting jobs, making several dollars more per hour than at his previous job.

Andrew's therapy—at least his therapy with me—ended around this time, as the number of hours he worked cut into his availability, and the new job got his father off his back about continuing his sessions. But his real therapy—his relationship with his new boss—continued. And this is the part of Andrew's story that makes me smile. Several months later my friend said, "Hey, guess what I've got that kid doing—he's working on our new website. Turns out that he's done this stuff before; he's really good at it."

And even more recently: "Andrew's talking about going back to college . . . looks like I may lose him."

"Easy come, easy go," I replied. But really, it wasn't so easy at all. And even though my friend was losing a valuable employee, it looks now like Andrew has found his sense of direction.

Parents should know:

- Becoming relevant is really about giving young people a sense of direction, an optimism and faith that they can find purpose in the adult world.
- Sometimes this sense of purpose will be different from yours (or from what you would have wanted for them!). Parents and career counselors often advise the practical option—the one leading directly to a "good job." But if your transitioner has no energy or excitement about that path, it may become a dead end. Look for your transitioner's energy, his or her "campfire in the cave," and encourage them to find a way to build upon that. Without energy behind what they want to accomplish, transitioners will sputter and stall.
- Parents can help teach struggling transitioners find a direction by (1) replacing a negative bubble world (a situation with few responsibilities and few consequences) with a positive holding environment (like a gap year or a work opportunity); (2) asking themselves, "What am I modeling about adult life?" Making *your own* life more meaningful can be an inspiration for your transitioner; and (3) setting up mentoring opportunities so they can start to interact with other adults (besides you!) to practice what it means to live in the new realm of adulthood.

Part III

How Parents Can Help

*What You Can
(and Can't)
Do for Your Kid*

Chapter 7

How Guilty
Should You Feel?

Own Your Role—and Move Past It

I have an adult client, Maggie, with whom I've worked as a parenting consultant and psychotherapist for several years. She has three adult children, two of whom are grown and thriving with young families of their own, and one who now, in his midtwenties, after several false starts, is finally launching. Maggie and her husband, with my support and coaching, did a good job of getting their youngest son out of the basement and into the driver's seat of his own life.

Maggie and I have continued meeting on a semi-regular basis, but our focus has shifted from her youngest to her thirty-something oldest, with whom she has long had a strained relationship. He lives in the same city as Maggie, is married with three young children, and has developed into a successful financial professional (a field that makes good use of his tendencies toward OCD and inclinations toward precision and control). The problem for Maggie—the one we spend most of our time examining—is that this son is an inveterate bully. When she visits her grandchildren, he imposes stringent rules and guidelines that she must follow. Some of them make sense, such as restrictions regarding which foods and snacks are acceptable and what video content is appropriate. Lots of responsible parents set guidelines for grandparents. (As my son said to me, concerning treats and snacks when his boys were young: "We pay the dentist bills; we decide the menu.")

Maggie's son, however, takes the business of grandparent management to a new level. For example, when she babysits, she is required to send hourly text "reports" on how the children are faring. When she takes them somewhere, she must have GPS tracking enabled on her phone, so he can monitor their whereabouts (and heaven forbid that her GPS icon appears at an ice cream shop or at a children's park that her son deems "dangerous"). Not surprising, whenever her grandparenting displeases him in the least, he upbraids her sternly—in a fashion she finds humiliating.

"Why in the world do you put up with such behavior?" I asked.

"Because those children mean the world to me," she countered.

"But that doesn't mean you have to tolerate being treated so disrespectfully," I pointed out. And that's when we get to the real story, the one forever in the background—the story of her guilt.

"When he was in elementary and middle school," she began, "I insisted he attend a traditional parochial school. I did that because my own parents would have disapproved had I sent him to public school. This school recruited students to assist in

religious services, and we strongly encouraged him to participate. He protested, but we felt strongly that being an active part
of the school and church community would be good for him. It
turned out, several years later, that we should have listened. One
of the clergy was accused of sexual abuse. We don't know if our
son was abused, and he has refused to discuss those times whenever we've broached the subject."

"But how does that explain your current relationship?" I asked.

"Well, we felt horrible and completely responsible. He was in
therapy all through high school, on account of what his therapist
called 'depressive acting out.' I've never gotten over the feeling
that we did this to him."

What happened at home during high school was this: Whenever her son acted up and pushed the limits, as high schoolers
are wont to do, railing against his parents for "ruining his life,"
Maggie didn't process his adolescent rage rationally or objectively; she just took it. In a semiconscious way, she felt she
deserved it.

Fast-forward to the present. Maggie has a warm, loving relationship with her grandchildren and a relationship with her son
that, while superficially serviceable, is haunted by the unresolved dynamics of adolescence. And poor Maggie—speaking, I
believe, for many parents in comparable situations—is saddled
with an unresolved question: "How guilty *should* I feel?"

That's a terrific question. After all, parenting is among the
class of human endeavors positively doomed to generate the experience of failure. We start out as new parents convinced that
we will correct the mistakes our own parents made—we will get

it *right* where others have gotten it wrong. But as one of my mentors once said, "The surest cure for perfectionism is parenting!"

Parenting humbles, pure and simple.

And if the goal of parenting is to launch our children into happy and successful adulthood, then parents of struggling transitioners may be the humblest of them all.

Is It All My Fault?

There are two mistaken assumptions I commonly encounter when working with parents. The first is that the parent is responsible for his or her transitioner's developmental difficulties. These are the parents whose nagging sense of guilt for not being good enough or for having gone through a divorce or for having battled with anxiety or depression or substance abuse themselves leaves them with a vague and pervasive fear that *they* are somehow the underlying reason that their son or daughter is struggling. And because they feel responsible, they feel obligated to make things right.

This is an erroneous assumption of parental *guilt*, and it is never helpful.

The second mistaken assumption I frequently encounter is, ironically, the opposite: that parents, because they have offered support and advice with the purest of intentions, bear *no* responsibility for the shortsightedness, poor decisions, and dysfunctional entitlement that their struggling transitioners exhibit. Their kids "are who they are," and parents can't do anything to change it. This is an assumption of parental irrelevance, and it is similarly unhelpful.

In this chapter, we will accomplish two things. First, we will relieve you of counterproductive guilt. Your transitioner may be struggling and you may have had some role in that, but you can also help change that dynamic for the better. And second, we will encourage you to take a closer, more objective look at the subtle ways that you may participate in and reinforce (however inadvertently) your transitioner's counterproductive behavior. Sometimes you may not even realize the subtle ways you are reinforcing the very behavior you want to change.

The first objective has to do with *letting go of guilt*; the second has to do with *accepting responsibility*.

These two are vastly different mind-sets.

So: Just how guilty *should* you feel? I'll answer that question by introducing you to Jack and Myrna, who are the parents of twenty-three-year-old Gordon, a transitioner as responsibility-challenged as any I've ever worked with. Later in this chapter I'll point out significant ways that Jack and Myrna's parenting contributed to Gordon's lack of progress, but for now I'll tell you about their guilt. Jack and Myrna had a rocky relationship, and after fourteen years of marriage and several years of unrelenting conflict, decided that they would divorce. They consulted a therapist, who coached them on how best to inform their children—Gordon, twelve years old at the time; an older sister, Frances, sixteen; and a younger sister, Helen, age nine. This led to each of the children consulting therapists, which brought Gordon to my office.

Like every therapist who works with children and/or adolescents, I have supported many young clients through the breakup
of their parents' marriage and the loss of their familiar family
life. But this one was different. Jack and Myrna spent the next
six years moving forward and then stepping back from the divorce process, whipsawing their children's emotional adjustment to an unpredictable and constantly changing situation.
One month, Jack and Myrna were proceeding to meet with their
lawyers and hash out all the issues attendant to dissolving a
marriage, only to retreat from this process several months later
with the stated intention of exploring possible reconciliation.
They couldn't live with each other and couldn't live without each
other. For the children, and certainly for my client, Gordon, it
was like trying to gain secure footing on a trampoline.

Six full years later, when Gordon was eighteen and on the
verge of heading off to college, Jack and Myrna finally gave up
their well-intended but disastrous efforts to reconcile and sur-
rendered, largely out of marital exhaustion, to the process of divorce. To their considerable credit, they conducted themselves
throughout and subsequently with civility and mutual consideration. They were one of those couples who did much better divorced than married.

As their parenting consultant during Gordon's adolescence, I
can assure you that spending time with Jack and Myrna was
painful. Setting aside speculation about their individual under-
currents of guilt regarding their marital disaster, they both acknowledged the effect that their unrelenting misery and conflict
had on Gordon, particularly during his teenage years. Their

attention to Gordon's behavioral and academic challenges was often spotty, their discipline was inconsistent, and they frequently undermined each other.

I had serious misgivings when Gordon headed off to college but crossed my fingers and wished him the best. Fast-forward three years, and I was contacted by Gordon's parents around the time he turned twenty-one. By that time, he was floundering, already on his third college. Throughout the course of his three-college roller-coaster ride, Gordon had exhibited the executive function and administrative responsibility of an immature teenager, as his parents bailed him out of one mess after another, time after time. Too often, the unmistakable motive for their parenting was not to support and challenge Gordon to learn from mistakes but to ameliorate their collective guilt for having prepared him so poorly for growing up.

So again, the question: How guilty should they (you) feel? The answer is fairly simple: Do your darnedest to set your guilt aside. Guilt *never* helps in parenting. Instead, it gets in the way, clouding your judgment and sending you off on a quest to make yourself feel better, rather than focusing on what your transitioner needs *now*. Guilt is a self-involved, often self-indulgent emotion. There's nothing you can do about the past except to acknowledge it and move on. When Maggie finally came to terms with her imperfect parenting—not being attuned enough to an unhappy middle schooler—she was able to see her now-grown son's adult behavior in a more realistic light: simply as postponed adolescent behavior, rather than as a punishment she deserved. From this new perspective, she engineered an adult-to-adult conversation with her son about their relationship, laying down clear expectations for civility and mutual respect. Things dramatically improved once she began parenting with her judgment rather than with her guilt.

So get it off your chest. You didn't spend enough time with your kids. You should have insisted upon more family dinners together. You should have helped more (or perhaps less) with their homework. You were too hard on them and should have allowed more time for play and creativity. Or you overindulged them, making their life too easy. Maybe you shouldn't have gone back to work. Certainly you could have tried harder at your marriage. Maybe you shouldn't have had that cocktail or two every evening. Maybe you failed to model discipline and hard work. Or perhaps you worked too hard and failed to demonstrate that adulthood can be fun. Whatever it is that you did too much or too little of, get it off your chest.

And get over it. Because you're not helping yourself or, more important, your kid.

Instead, focus on the task at hand. What do you need to do *differently* to help your transitioner learn the essential lessons of growing up? Ask yourself what your child needs from you *now*. The first step in addressing this question—once you've set aside your guilt—is to take a look in the mirror and ask yourself the real question, which is: What about *my* behavior? How might my *current* parenting be contributing to the difficulties that my transitioner is having with growing up?

The good news about looking in the mirror and discovering how you may be contributing to your transitioner's situation is that you *can* do something about this. I've mentioned repeatedly how helpless parents can feel. The best thing about discovering what you can change in your own behavior is that it makes you feel *less helpless*. It gives you a small measure of power and confidence that you can move things in a positive direction.

To illustrate how parents can unwittingly, even with the best intentions, contribute to their transitioner's immature thinking, let me tell you a personal story. It makes me laugh now, but it wasn't funny at the time.

Who's the Lunatic?

Here's my story. Once, when my daughter was an eighteen-year-old high school senior, she had the day off from school and asked if she could use my car to get together with friends. "Sure," I said. "You'll just need to drop me at my office at noon, and then Mom can pick me up when I'm done." Simple enough. Except she came back after conferring with her friends and asked if instead she could drop me off at eleven A.M. I thought for a few minutes about what I needed to get done and replied that her timetable wouldn't work for me. She could drop me off at noon and then the car would be hers for the rest of the day.

What did she do? You probably know the answer. She argued. "Why not? It's just one hour's difference; noon will be too late," and so on. I calmly held my ground and her exasperation grew. Finally she blurted out: "Honestly! You and Mom act like you *own* the cars!"

I couldn't believe what I was hearing, because (of course) we *did* own the cars. *And* the house, and the phones, and . . . well, you get it.

I instantly regretted what I said next. "Either you're putting me on . . . or you're a lunatic!"

She stomped away and later dropped me off at noon.

I thought about that bizarre interchange for the longest time. How could a bright, seemingly mature high school senior have such a warped understanding of basic economics? This question rolled around in the back of my brain for at least a week before an explanation occurred to me. As a therapist, I have long held the belief that so-called crazy behavior—in this case, her nutty statement about the cars—is crazy only as long as we fail to grasp the full psychological context in which it occurs. Once we identify the (often invisible) context of assumptions and beliefs and emotions that gave rise to the irrational behavior, it begins to make sense.

Here's what I figured out. When I grew up, before the age of democratic parenting, there was never any question whatsoever about who owned the cars in our family or whose agenda took priority. It was the parents' world, pure and simple. If I had an important event on a given Saturday morning and my dad had a golf game—well, I either hitchhiked or arranged for a ride with a friend. My parents weren't the least bit neglectful; it was just the way things worked in those days.

I, becoming a parent in the halcyon new age of the post-sixties, resolved that my children would always know that they were taken seriously and that their agendas counted within the family. And yes (this is still a little embarrassing), I treated the cars as if they were community property. I never said so explicitly and would have recognized it as a nutty idea if I had. It took my daughter's frustration that particular morning to put *my* lunacy—treating the family cars as community property—into words.

She wasn't the lunatic. I was.

What's needed here—and this is the first task for many of the parents I coach—is an honest, soul-searching assessment of the role we have played, and continue to play, in constructing and sustaining the psychological worlds in which our children live, the worlds they take for granted. In some cases, this role is explicit and obvious, and therefore easy to identify. But in many instances, the role we play is not so obvious. We find ourselves unexpectedly confronted with behavior that leaves us scratching our heads, wondering: *What's wrong with them? How can they be so irresponsible, so entitled, so unappreciative?* When this happens, we frequently find ourselves responding with irritation, resentment, and critical judgment. But here I am reminded of the oft-quoted line "We have met the enemy and he is us!"

Looking in the Mirror

There are three specific ways that parents influence their transitioners, often without being aware that they are doing so: parental expectations, parental modeling, and the creation of family culture. If you're fortunate enough to have an emerging adult who is thriving in his or her quest for adulthood, it's likely that these three factors have contributed to their success. But if you have a struggling transitioner, there's an equally good chance that one or more of these factors may be contributing to his or her struggles. Let's look at each in turn.

Parental Expectations

Parental expectations exert a tremendous and largely constructive influence on child development. Expectations tell children what is desirable and undesirable, what is virtuous and worthy of their energies, and what is possible for them to achieve. Children unfortunate enough to have parents who expect little from them frequently achieve little, both in character development and behavioral accomplishments. Expectations are the guideposts of child development, and without them, children are lost.

But there's another side to this coin with struggling transitioners. When parents find transitioners dropping the ball and remaining stuck in less-than-responsible patterns of adolescence, their expectations often become saturated with anxiety, creating the unintended result of an adolescent-style power struggle. I recently met with a parent whose son was three credits short of finishing his college education. In fact, the twenty-three-year-old had been three credits short for more than a year, and this drove his father crazy. Every time he saw or talked to his son, he brought it up: "Have you signed up for that course yet? You know that they have weekend and evening classes?"

The son consequently put more energy into avoidance and irritation with his father than into finishing his education. I advised the dad: "Let it go. He'll encounter the consequences of not finishing his degree soon enough. Let the real world do the parenting for you." By fixating so intently on this matter, the father unwittingly deflected his son's attention from the dilemma of completing his education, focusing him instead on resisting his father's control. The son eventually completed his degree, but I have no doubt that his well-intended father delayed, rather than accelerated, the process.

When it comes to conveying your expectations to your transitioner, there are three important principles to keep in mind.

- **Principle 1.** Pick your battles. Don't waste your breath on issues (like those last three credits for graduation) that in time will likely take care of themselves on their own. Save your expectations for important things—core family values, issues of ethical integrity, matters related to health and physical safety, and the like. If your children know you'll nag them about everything, they will be reluctant to come to you about anything.

- **Principle 2.** Talk about big-picture goals, not day-to-day objectives. Saying to your home-for-the-summer college student, "I want you to go down to Wegmans today and fill out a job application," is likely to trigger a power struggle, but if you express your expectations as a principle and leave the particulars open to negotiation, you're giving them some agency. For example: "We expect you to do *something* constructive this summer. It doesn't matter to us what it is. You could go down to Wegmans and see if they're hiring, you could go over to the golf course and caddy, you could check with your friends who are working and see if any of their employers are hiring, you could sign up for college credits and throw in some volunteer work. It's up to you, but doing nothing—that's *not* on the menu!" Expectations are best expressed at a macro-level of general principle, rather than at a micro-level of a particular choice or option.

- **Principle 3.** Don't confuse your preferences with your expectations. Allow me to illustrate the difference. When I had transitioner-age children, I *preferred* that they run or exercise on a regular basis, meditate, wear clean underwear, keep their dorm room or apartment reasonably tidy, recycle, read, pay attention to national and local news, and vote. I preferred that they *not* play video games until two A.M., work late shifts at a restaurant, dye their hair blue and green, get tattoos or body piercings, listen to offensive music, have sex with strangers, do Jell-O shots, and a host of other things too numerous to mention. These were just some of my preferences.

My expectations were another matter entirely, and related mostly to matters where I had a legitimate stake. I expected them, while at school, to attend classes, do their work, and learn. When living under my roof, I expected them to conduct themselves with civility, comply with my (very reasonable, in my opinion) house rules, abstain from using substances while driving, and be involved full time in either schooling, work, or some combination of the two. I'm sure I expected a few other things, too, but you get the picture. My advice: Save your expectations for the big things—the things that will shape the future, and the values that you consider nonnegotiable.

Another way parental expectations can become part of the problem is if they reflect only the *parents'* wishes for the transitioner's future, without taking into account the transitioner's own interests and aspirations.

This is what happened with Gordon and his parents. Gordon graduated from high school in spite of his immaturity and was accepted, by virtue of his dedicated tutors and superior standardized test scores, into several four-year colleges. What was he hoping to study? An avid gamer with strong programming skills, Gordon wanted to become a video game designer. His parents, Jack and Myrna, saw this as adolescent fantasy. If they were going to pay for college, they wanted him to study something that would make him, in their view, a grown-up. They convinced Gordon to register as a business major, on the premise that a business degree would prepare him more adequately for the adult world, whereas they believed video game design would only perpetuate his adolescent avoidance of growing up.

We could debate whether they were correct, but that would miss the more important question—which was how their expectations impacted Gordon. When I met him in therapy, a year and a half after he had been booted from the business program, he lamented that his parents didn't seem to know or care who he really was. This wasn't true. They cared deeply, in fact perhaps too much. But to Gordon it *seemed* they didn't care, because they wouldn't take his views and aspirations seriously. Jack's and Myrna's expectations, for all their good intentions, had unintentionally become a force of discouragement and alienation in their relationship with their son.

It's important to remember that transitioners, even when they seem to defy and ignore their parents' expectations, remain acutely aware of them. And they are even more acutely aware of the degree to which those expectations make space for their own fledgling identities and authenticity. My advice: If your transitioner wants to design video games, encourage him to enroll in computer science (which, by the way, is what Gordon is studying now) and expect him to take his studies seriously. If she wants to become a pop star, offer musical training, but again, expect that she take it seriously. It is far more important that your transitioner learn to pursue a goal—*any* goal—with initiative and commitment than it is that he or she makes the "right" choice in the eyes of his or her parents.

With struggling transitioners, parents often *do* know what would be best. Indeed, our best intentions lead us to ramp up our expectations when we see him or her wandering off in unproductive directions. But sometimes these certainties and good intentions lead us to miss the authentic nature of a beautiful child who is struggling to emerge. There is a litmus test that can be applied to parental expectations, a test that reveals whether these will ultimately prove to be supportive or obstructive for the child's growth and development. That litmus test is this: *How accurately do your expectations match the talents and aspirations of your child, and how congruent are those expectations with your child's understanding of him- or herself?*

In other words, how is your child likely to *experience* your expectations? The transitioner, whether you like it or not, is the final arbiter of whether your expectations are helpful or obstructive. When you fail to take into account your transitioner's first-person experience of your expectations and, more important, of what matters to *him or her* in life, you run the risk of obstructing the learning process in which young people evolve and discover themselves.

Parental Modeling

The old saying "Do as I say, not as I do" is often invoked as a joke, because of its patent unreasonableness. But this phrase is an inevitable part of parenting. Why? Because it's a matter of human nature, as most of us are more acutely aware of how we *ought* to behave as opposed to how we *actually* behave. Practically speaking, this means that a significant percentage of the modeling we do as parents is out of our awareness, which suggests another important question: "What does my own behavior and lifestyle convey to my transitioner about achievement, self-care, perfectionism, substance use, flexibility, integrity, honesty, and so on? And in a more general sense, what does my life situation say to my transitioner about the business of becoming an adult?"

Remember Andrew from chapter 6? He was the boy who looked at his parents' joyless lives and concluded that adulthood had nothing to offer. This is not to accuse his poor parents, who undoubtedly were suffering themselves and were more or less doing the best they could. Yet their situation serves as a reminder that an important part of parenting is to do our level best to live meaningful, fulfilling, and ethical lives ourselves— to model the sort of lives we want our children to live.

In many instances, the part we play in shaping our child's psychological world is subtle and implicit. Often I have met with parents who were perplexed by the intense pressure that their perfectionistic, highly stressed, overachieving children put on themselves.

"We don't understand it," these parents typically say. "We don't pressure her at all; we constantly tell her to ease up a little, to just do a good job. There's no need for perfection, but she pushes herself unnecessarily." The apparent mystery often disappears when I ask these same parents how much pressure they put on *themselves* in their careers, and they awkwardly acknowledge a closet perfectionism of their own. Even more ironically, they are often striving for perfection in their parenting. This is a classic "Do as I say, not as I do" scenario.

"You don't make excessive demands of your daughter," I point out to them. "You make these demands of yourselves. It's called modeling."

So whatever your personal proclivities—whether you work

too hard, complain too much, drink more than you should, or otherwise neglect your own mental health and well-being—know that you are modeling powerful messages for your children. They are watching.

Family Culture

Family culture refers to the unexpressed socially constructed world that parents create—often unconsciously—for their children. This is what I did for my daughter regarding the family cars. Each family communicates to its children a complex latticework of assumptions and expectations about the nature of living and how the world works. If your child has unspoken expectations that life is exciting, that opportunity exists, or that hard work pays off, this is probably due to your having created a family culture where these things are implicit. On the other hand, if your transitioner takes for granted that you will always be there to solve his or her problems or that the future will somehow magically take care of itself, it's quite possible that you had more to do with fostering these beliefs than you realize.

Let's think for a minute about my choice of the word *culture* to describe how families influence children. The formal study of this subject—cultural anthropology—has shown that cultures differ in terms of their tacit organizing assumptions about what matters in life and how the world works. This is evident in a culture's myths, language, art, societal organization, economics, religious beliefs, and so on. From a psychological and behavioral standpoint, there is no objective reality that all people share. In other words, *common sense* means exactly what the phrase denotes—sense-making (or meaning-making) that people of a given culture or society hold in common with one another.

Individual families differ from one another in much the same ways that cultures differ from one another. When we form a family, we create an implicit web of expectations and assumptions for our children concerning what matters in life, how people can and should behave, and how the world works. Most important for our purposes here, to some extent we create this web—like me with the family cars—with little or no awareness that we are doing so. For example, if we want to predict whether a particular child will grow up to be a reader, we can make a more accurate prediction based upon whether the family has a library in their home (an indication of deeper family culture) than if the parents made a point of reading to the child (a matter of conscious parenting). Family culture is deeper than the conscious intention and strategies we employ as parents, because it is the backdrop of parenting, the part of the iceberg that's beneath the water, unseen. It's the unconscious context that silently shapes the expectations that children form regarding how the world works.

Jack, Myrna, and Gordon, Revisited

Think back to Gordon, the struggling transitioner who had enrolled in a four-year university in the business school despite his video game designer aspirations. After a terrible first semester, his parents determined that the distractions of dormitory life were more than Gordon could handle and they set him up in a rental property, the second floor of a duplex, just off campus. They all agreed that this would give Gordon a quiet place to study, sufficiently removed from the hubbub of dormitory life. Only much later did his parents learn that this rental was in the middle of what local, disgruntled homeowners called "college row," hangout central for off-campus extracurricular shenanigans.

I got a call from Gordon's mother after she visited him, six weeks into the semester, and observed to her dismay that he had turned his apartment into a party house. In her words, she found the place trashed, with weeks of dirty laundry bundled into corners (which explained, sort of, the new clothing charges that had shown up on the credit card they had provided for emergencies). Upon her return home, Gordon's mother called me in a panic, fearing that her son was an emerging sociopath, thinking of no one but himself—wantonly disregarding the careful planning his parents had done to support this educational opportunity and exploiting their support to his own hedonistic ends.

But what did Gordon's mother do when she arrived at the scene of the crimes? For starters, she read him the riot act. She ranted up one side and down the other, told him what an irresponsible "little shit" he'd been, threatened to take him out of school, reiterated the purchasing restrictions that applied to the credit card, kicked out the college buddy who was crashing at his pad. And then *cleaned the apartment top to bottom and did his laundry!*

We can all agree that Gordon's behavior was adolescent to the max—irresponsible, entitled, and self-indulgent. But look at his behavior from a different point of view—not simply as output from an immature personality, but also as an expression of the family culture he grew up in. It's not surprising that Gordon had a history of similar behavior all the way back to junior high school. He "borrowed" personal items from other family members, treated family common space like his own private dumping ground, accumulated parking tickets and library fines with abandon, and neglected all manner of responsibilities when it suited him. Throughout this reckless history, his parents harangued, lectured, and "punished" him when they were angry enough, and paraded him through a series of therapists' offices. But—just as when his mother cleaned his apartment from top to bottom—he never encountered limits or real consequences and was never required to clean up his own messes.

Gordon sounds awful, but he wasn't. In fact, he was a sweet boy, if somewhat clueless and bewildered. He was always down on himself for his "screw-ups" and again and again resolved to straighten out his behavior. But when the inevitable next mess came to pass, he would sit in my office and shake his head in dismay at the foolishness of his own mysterious actions. He wasn't conning me; he was truly dismayed.

Family "Rules"

To understand this sort of behavior, think like a social scientist. Every social system has at least two sets of rules. There are the rules that are in the "handbook"—the "official" rules that everybody in the system can put into words. For example, at the mental health center where I had my first professional job, coffee break in the cafeteria was scheduled from 10:00 A.M. to 10:20 A.M. In my first week on the job, I left my office at 10:00 A.M. and returned at 10:20 A.M. on the dot. Then I noticed that most people sauntered down to the cafeteria around 9:55 A.M. and didn't return to their offices until nearly 10:30 A.M. "When exactly is the coffee break?" I asked the chief administrator near the end of my first week. "Ten A.M. to ten-twenty A.M.," she replied, with a perfectly straight face and no apparent recognition of the mischief in my question or the absurdity of her answer.

But this is the nature of both the human mind and social systems. We *think* we know the rules that govern our behavior. We can recite them if required. But the real rules—the concrete operational rules, as opposed to the abstract written rules—are something else indeed. And so it was in Gordon's family. The spoken rules (the ones his parents belabored time and time again) and the concrete rules (the ones that actually governed the way things played out) were miles apart.

"You may not take things that don't belong to you!" Except you could. You might get yelled at, but that turned out to be an acceptable price to pay.

"You are at college to get an education!" Except that was really more of a recommendation than a requirement. Gordon screwed up his academics royally and was reenrolled at a new college the following semester.

"You've got to take care of your personal effects!" Except a team of angry elves showed up periodically and left his apartment scrubbed and shiny, with all his clothes laundered and folded neatly in his drawers. Not a bad deal if you ask me, and we can hold Gordon only partly to blame for taking this absurd system for granted.

But before we all start throwing stones at Gordon and his parents, let's look at our own situations and the crazy ways we fail to make real the principles and guidelines we exhort our transitioners to heed. Here are some questions to ask yourself:

If your transitioner conducts his job search in slow motion, do you continue to cover bills (cell phone, car insurance, etc.) that might otherwise serve as real-world incentives for finding employment?

If your transitioner gets up late for work, do you go out of your way to make sure she gets to work on time, perhaps depriving her of an opportunity to learn how the real world values punctuality?

If your transitioner overdraws his checking account or neglects some other financial responsibility, do you obstruct the potential learning experience by bailing him out?

If your transitioner seems to have difficulty managing alcohol or other mood-altering substances, do you continue your own use unchanged?

If your transitioner treats your hard-earned tuition dollars as if money grew on trees, do you do the same?

If your transitioner deals with responsibilities in a passive fashion, do you step in and provide the missing initiative and energy in order to get the task accomplished?

If your transitioner is forgetful, do you provide an unsolicited reminder service?

If your transitioner fails to pay you back (as promised) for a loan, do you let her off with a lecture?

If your transitioner treats your home like his personal apartment, do you provide free maid service?

If your transitioner can't summon enough executive function to complete college or job applications, do you take on the role of executive secretary and make sure the task is completed?

If your transitioner complains of problems with anxiety or depression but won't seek or accept help, do you reinforce her helplessness by refusing to get supportive guidance for yourself?

If your transitioner treats you abusively, do you allow him to continue living in your home?

If your transitioner seems to be operating without a plan for the future, do you attempt to make plans for her?

If your transitioner needs self-care services (dentist, therapist, physician, etc.), do you compensate for an absence of initiative and good judgment by making those appointments for him?

My point isn't that you necessarily *shouldn't* be doing these things. But I want you to look at the *gap* between your family handbook (your spoken expectations, usually offered in the form of lectures) and your actual operating system (the messages conveyed by what actually happens). If you find a significant gap, you may be unwittingly participating in your transitioner's problem behavior.

How to fix this will depend upon your unique situation and individual child. Sometimes it's better to set aside the handbook when belaboring your expectations serves only to alienate your transitioner from influence. Other times—and this was the case for Gordon's parents—it's advisable to adjust your operating system such that it supports the life lessons you want your transitioner to learn. I can't tell you what you'll see when you look in the mirror, but by doing so, you'll be in a much better position to make the difficult parenting decisions that struggling transitioners require.

Gordon Grows Up

And Gordon? Last summer, several years after I last met with him and his parents, he scheduled an appointment. I had chalked up my work with him and his parents as a "therapeutic failure" on my part, since I had not succeeded in altering the negative, self-reinforcing patterns that kept them all stuck in an adolescent time warp. But the Gordon who showed up at my office was a different boy (actually, not a boy at all, but a twenty-four-year-old young man) from the one I had known. He was close to completing his computer science degree, and he was supporting himself financially (with the exception of college tuition, which his parents continued to fund). He worked part-time with a start-up cybersecurity firm, and he shared an apartment with several others who were now college graduates.

How did he manage such a significant turnaround? I asked.

He wasn't sure.

"I guess I just grew up," he volunteered.

But there was more to it, which became evident as he filled me in on recent family changes. Two years earlier, Gordon's older sister had had twins, his parents' first grandchildren. His mother was smitten, falling instantly in love with her two new granddaughters. This resulted in shifting her focus and energy away from the task of managing Gordon to the deeply rewarding role of helping out her daughter and grandparenting her daughter's baby girls. Thanks to Gordon's two new nieces, the underlying rules that had silently governed Gordon's life and family relationships necessarily changed. No one came to his rescue when he overslept for work or missed a registration deadline for school. No magic elves cleaned his apartment or did his laundry. He first learned how to clean up these problems by himself, and then gradually how to avoid them altogether. Gordon, it turned out, wasn't the "little shit" his mother had declared him to be, nor was he the "screw-up" he took himself to be.

He was just someone who played by the rules.

Parents should know:

- Every honest parent can acknowledge some guilt associated with their former parenting, but guilt won't help you or your child move forward. Acknowledge your past imperfections and let them go. Instead, take an honest and objective look at how your current parenting practices may unwittingly contribute to or reinforce your transitioner's problematic behavior.

- Don't confuse your preferences concerning minor behaviors with your well-grounded expectations concerning important, life-altering issues. Communicate those expectations clearly.

- Model the behaviors in yourself that you say you want your transitioner to exhibit.

- Take a step back and look at your family system as a "culture," complete with implicit prescriptions and prohibitions. If you're too immersed in your family culture to see this clearly, ask for honest feedback from a close friend or trusted associate.

- Be honest with yourself about gaps between the "official" rules in your family "handbook" (the ones everyone can recite) and the unspoken, concrete rules that actually govern how things play out. Aligning your spoken rules and expectations with your actual rules and expectations helps parents and transitioners get on the same page.

Chapter 8

Untangling Boundaries

Reshaping the Relationship,
Not Fixing Behaviors

R emember Nick and his parents from chapter 1? When they came to see me, he had been living at home for a year after bombing out of college. The agreement struck with his parents was that Nick would commit to a combination of work and school that equated to full-time employment. Accordingly, Nick got himself a part-time job at a hardware/garden center and signed up for two general studies courses at the local community college. At first things went reasonably well, with Nick attending classes in the morning, and working afternoon shifts at the hardware store, where he progressed from lifting and hauling to customer service.

Before long, however, things began falling apart. Nick began closing a local bar with several coworkers after his evening work shifts, frequently arriving home at two or three in the morning. It became increasingly evident to his parents that Nick was having difficulty managing his alcohol use, as his knocking about the kitchen and stumbling up the stairs frequently woke them. They had repeatedly "talked to" (i.e., lectured at and argued with) Nick about his alcohol use to no avail. Nick seemed to have found a second family with the late-night tavern regulars—the tavern having become a bubble world to which Nick escaped—and he was resistant to change. His "citizenship" at home deteriorated, too, as Nick became increasingly inconsiderate and disrespectful, regressively resembling the surly teenager he had once been.

Not surprising, Nick's commitment to his college classes declined in similar fashion. Keeping such late hours and with hangovers to sleep off, he missed morning classes with regularity. Nick objected strenuously to his parents' academic supervision, claiming repeatedly that he had things under control. But when he finally received his grades, a C- and an incomplete told another story. The incomplete, Nick rationalized, was not his fault. The professor, he maintained, had an accent that was impossible to understand, and thus Nick had "dropped" the class— by which he meant he had stopped attending. However, he hadn't gone through the formal process of petitioning the registrar's office —thus the incomplete. It was around this time, with tension and conflict among them almost unbearable, that his parents insisted on the three of them consulting a therapist.

When I first met with Nick and his parents, they resembled the classic picture of a family with an oppositional defiant adolescent. For one thing, Nick seemed oblivious to his parents' personal boundaries, often showing little regard for their belongings. When he invited friends over to watch a Sunday-afternoon football game, his parents later found the family room a mess, cluttered with snack trays and beer cans, complete with crumbled chips in the seat cushions. The stock of premium microbrew beers that his parents purchased for their own (modest) consumption was depleted from time to time. The special granola that Dad stocked for his breakfast was occasionally sacrificed to Nick's late-night snacking. And on one occasion, when Dad couldn't find his heirloom Zippo lighter (a treasured item that had belonged to *his* father), it turned up in the wash in Nick's pants pocket. His parents' requests that he respect their belongings were met more often with surly sighs than with apologies. Nick was firm in his insistence that his parents stay out of his business, but seemed oblivious to the fact that respect for boundaries needed to be reciprocal.

Nick objected to what he labeled his parents' "micromanagement." But this complaint merely deflected attention from the real issue—that Nick himself was doing a poor job of managing his behavior and his responsibilities. He missed classes, managed his sleep needs poorly, drank too much, took his parents' good graces for granted, and avoided any meaningful planning for the future.

Nick's parents—Seth and Renée—tried to shape up his behavior with reminders and admonitions, but this left Nick bristling at their disapproval and judgment, further straining their relationship. His mother, citing Nick's lack of initiative in lobbying for more hours at work or looking for a second job, would often leave want ads on the breakfast table with plausible job openings circled in red. When his "sleeping in and missing class" behavior began, she would leave notes for him at night, reminding him of his morning schedule. When this failed to change his behavior, she did her tactful best to wake and get him off to morning classes. In other words, there were a host of responsibilities that *should* have been owned and managed by Nick but that he consistently neglected. Mom and Dad, seeing this, instinctively attempted to prod and coach him into managing the business he neglected. As much as they longed to treat Nick like an adult, they increasingly felt like they were once again parenting an adolescent.

When Nick first came home from his failed college experience, his mother's ministrations had indeed proved helpful. For example, he was intimidated by the initial process of enrolling in classes at the community college, and she had helped by researching course offerings and walking him through the when, where, and how of registration. Nick needed help at that moment, and he was grateful for her assistance. But as he lost momentum, her continued efforts to help became non grata and served only to strengthen his belief that his parents were micromanaging. At one point, when I had begun to meet with Nick regularly, he complained that her efforts to have him research vocational training or associates degree programs were an example of her "trying to control my life!"

Dad's efforts to help Nick were received in the same way— initially with appreciation but eventually with irritation and resentment. Early on, Dad arranged several "business lunches" with Nick to help him set goals for himself. When it became clear that Nick was having trouble following through, his father drew up a "business plan," bullet-pointing things he believed Nick needed to do in order to take control of his future:

- Exercise and get back into shape
- Open a savings account and put aside some money
- Balance checkbook
- Get back on a healthy sleep-wake cycle
- Meet with a college adviser to discuss long-range educational goals

Later, once Nick had settled into a pattern of spending afterwork hours at the tavern, his dad repeatedly attempted to talk to him about his drinking. And when he came across a credit card statement that detailed Nick's tavern expenditures (remember, Nick occasionally bought rounds for the house), his dad hit the roof. By the time they came to see me, it was apparent that the net effect of their efforts to influence Nick was at best for naught and at worst counterproductive.

Nick's parents were doing what caring parents do when they see their transitioner making poor choices and wrong turns. They tried to fix Nick's behavior in all the usual ways. They gave suggestions, made recommendations, offered hints, and lectured. In short, they offered guidance. But Nick wasn't taking it, and that was the problem. In fact, the more they tried to help, the more tension and conflict developed in the relationship. And the greater the tension and conflict between Nick and his parents, the more he insulated himself from their influence. He deflected and deceived, he rejected their advice, he dug in his heels about doing things "his way." The more they tried to set Nick straight, the more he shut them out.

It's a fair assessment to say that Nick's overall level of responsibility and self-management more resembled that of an unruly teenager than that of a twenty-two-year-old emerging adult. But it wasn't just Nick's behavior that had regressed to adolescent status—*it was the entire relationship.* As much as Nick had fallen into thinking and behaving like a teenager, his parents had descended the same slippery slope, resembling again the parents of a teenager. His unsuccessful undermanaging was mirrored by their unsuccessful overmanaging. Areas of responsibility that rightly should have been Nick's to deal with—managing his finances, looking for full-time employment, investigating educational opportunities—had somehow ended up in their hands. What should have been his own worry and concern had somehow become theirs.

In the parlance of family therapy, Nick's family had become a nest of tangled and confused *boundaries.* When we first met Nick and his parents in chapter 1, I raised the question of what parents in situations like this are supposed to do. How can they help get Nick going, motivate him, and help him find direction? How can they get Nick to relate to them in a more age-appropriate fashion? The answer is NOT, as we've seen, to continue parenting as if they are the parents of an adolescent. Continuing to provide Nick with material support while nagging him for more grown-up behavior (which is what we do with adolescents) serves only to entrench adolescent thinking and behavior by reinforcing the dynamics of an adolescent-parent relationship.

Seth and Renée experienced firsthand the futility of trying to change Nick. As is true of many parents of struggling transitioners, their son's behavior trapped them in an adolescent parenting relationship. They labored under the mistaken assumption that their relationship with Nick couldn't mature until *Nick* matured. But they were wrong, and this is the key: Trying to change Nick's behavior directly was doomed to fail. They simply weren't in control of Nick's behavior—he was an adult (in age if not in actions). But changing the tangled boundaries of their parent-child relationship—*that* they could do.

Relational Boundaries: My Business, Your Business, and Our Business

What exactly do we mean by the term *boundaries?* In common parlance, *boundary* refers to the limits of something, such as the border of a geographical territory. In human psychology, boundaries refer to the limits of personal territory, whether that territory is physical (my home or my office), behavioral (my responsibilities), or experiential (my thoughts and feelings).

For many people, what first comes to mind when we speak of boundaries are barriers, those unspoken but unmistakable ways that people limit their availability and keep other people out of their business. But boundaries are about much more than keeping people out. In fact, they are really about the opposite— they're about how we let people in. Boundaries refer to the ways that we organize our relationships—how we establish what is *my business*, what is *your business*, and what is our *shared business*—and this process is what allows us to have meaningful relationships with one another. A good way to summarize this is to think of boundaries as *regulating* our relationships, in the sense that "good fences make good neighbors."

In relationships with clearly defined roles—teacher-student, employer-employee, therapist-client, and so on—boundaries tend to be prescribed and unambiguous. But in most of our ordinary day-to-day relationships, boundaries are established through a subtle and often unconscious process that resembles *negotiation*.

Here's an everyday example. I used to have a neighbor who was also my doctor. Without ever discussing it explicitly, we worked out a relationship where I never raised medical questions when we met across our backyard fence, though he was free to do so if he had information that he thought might benefit me. I let him determine when to be my doctor and when to be my neighbor. Please note that I'm not suggesting that there is one correct way to handle this; rather, I am saying that we negotiated our doctor-patient and neighbor-neighbor boundaries in a fashion we were both comfortable with. We talked about our yards, occasionally about our children, and in passing, about the weather. We didn't talk about our marriages, our personal frustrations, or our emotional lives, among many other things. And medical issues were never raised at my initiative. The boundary my neighbor and I negotiated didn't keep us *out* of each other's lives; it did just the opposite, organizing how we could be connected in a way that worked for both of us.

As a general rule, when interpersonal boundaries are clear and consensual, relationships tend to go smoothly. On the other hand, when these boundaries are contested or ambiguous—as they became with Nick and his parents—confusion and conflict are almost certain to follow. This conflict and confusion inevitably characterize the relationships of struggling transitioners and their parents. Nick *ought* to be managing his business—his responsibilities, his obligations, his preparation for an adult future—but he is not. And Seth and Renée, caring as desperately as they do about Nick's future, regularly step across the boundary and attempt to "help." Whereas this natural parenting impulse works, more or less, with children and adolescents, it often becomes part of the problem when one's children are in the transitional years between adolescence and emerging adulthood.

Boundaries and Development

What do relationship boundaries have to do with child development?

Consider the following scene, which I witnessed in my daughter's kitchen (the same daughter mentioned in the previous chapter, only now she has a good job and four little girls—and *she* owns the cars!). Four-year-old Clara stands by the kitchen door, dressing to go outdoors. It's winter, so she has on her warm coat, but she is wrestling with the zipper, struggling to manipulate the doohickey into the zipper's slot so that she can zip up her jacket. As she wrestles with the task, her mother stands by, calmly observing and offering to help, but accepting Clara's insistence that she can do it herself.

It's taken mother and daughter a bit of work to arrive at this placid moment. Several weeks ago, when Clara first decided that she could do the zipper by herself, she actually couldn't, and the time demands of getting her out of the house and off to pre-school did not allow Mom to wait indefinitely while Clara fumbled. Efforts at coaching were met with resistance, and more than once, when Mom stepped in assertively with "Here, let me do that for you," Clara threw herself onto the floor in teary protest.

But that time has passed. Clara has gradually mastered the skill, and Mom patiently grants her the minute or so necessary for Clara to complete the job herself. This small moment contains in microcosm the story of child development, and it tells that story in terms of the evolving *boundary* of the parent-child relationship. When Clara took over the task of zipping up her winter coat, she and her mother were engaged in a subtle form of negotiation about the boundary of their relationship—the question of whose business is what. Zipping up the coat used to be Mom's business; now it's Clara's. We tend to think of child development as something that occurs solely *within* the child, but it is also something that occurs *between* the child and the parent. It's not just Clara's hand-eye coordination that developmentally inched forward when she mastered the zipper, but the parent-child relationship as well.

Over the next twenty years or so, this reorganization of their relationship will be repeated hundreds—perhaps thousands—of times as responsibilities transfer from one side of the boundary to the other. This is the nature of parenting and child development. When our children are infants, we dress them, whereas when they become toddlers, they begin to dress themselves. When they are in elementary school, we arrange their playdates, but by high school, they manage their own social lives. In each instance, psychological and behavioral responsibilities migrate from the parents' to the child's side of the boundary as both the child and the relationship itself mature.

This process often occurs smoothly, but sometimes it doesn't. There can be contention, confusion, and conflict about whose business is what. If you're a parent, you know that children often neglect responsibilities that they are fully capable of managing, and that this accounts for some of the periodic challenges and frustrations of parenting. Confronted with a child who fails to manage his or her rightful business, parents typically step over the boundary and get involved in managing the child's behavior. They nag until the dog is walked, the room is neatened, or the homework is completed. And because most children have a developmental aversion to parental supervision and a natural desire for autonomy and self-determination, sooner or later they take ownership, more or less, of the tasks in question. This push and pull—this back-and-forth negotiation of ownership and responsibility—is the essence of what it means to parent.

The Natural History of Parenting: Supervising, Negotiating, Consulting

If child development involves the evolution of parent-child boundaries, the same can be said about parenting. In fact, parenting evolves through stages that correspond to the evolving boundaries of the relationship between parent and child. In the first stage of parenting—supervision/caretaking—the child's business *is* the parent's business. Even when little Clara decided she wanted to zip up her winter coat by herself, it was her mother's responsibility to oversee the learning process and decide when it was appropriate to cede management of the task to the child. And if several years from now, Clara decides she doesn't want to do her homework, it will be her parents' responsibility to sit her down at the kitchen table and make sure she learns how to manage her assignments. This is the essence of stage one parenting, supervision/caretaking: Parents hold the final responsibility for the child's developmental progress.

By the time Clara becomes a teenager, however, her parents will discover that this kind of direct supervision is less effective and in many instances may lead to conflict and resentment. When this happens, as it inevitably does with adolescents, her parents will shift gears and begin to rely on a mode of parenting that looks more like *negotiation* than supervision. They will set up quid pro quo arrangements (for example, managing schoolwork = weekend privileges) and will exert their influence by holding Clara accountable and conferring privileges when she manages responsibly and consequences when she does not. This is quite different from direct oversight and supervision, because it concedes that the adolescent is more of an independent decision-maker than she was as a child.

At this point, her parents will have entered the second stage of parenting—negotiation and accountability—where parental influence is exerted through a more collaborative back-and-forth process. And what will be negotiated throughout adolescence, in countless ways, is the question of whose business is what.

Let me give a personal example of what I mean by boundary negotiation. When Clara's mother—my daughter—was in seventh grade, I came into the kitchen one morning to find her completing homework left over from the previous evening. "Homework is not to be done in the morning," I pronounced in a fatherly tone. To which she replied, "Do you have a problem with my grades?"

"No," I answered (because she was, in fact, an excellent student).

"Well," she declared, "when you have a problem with my grades, then you can tell me when to do my homework!" I blustered for a minute, discovered that I didn't really have an answer, and then conceded the point. I was outnegotiated by a thirteen-year-old, because she was right. She was declaring that her homework was *her* business, not mine, and the bottom line of her successful academic performance proved her point.

When all goes well during the teen years (and, of course, in the case of struggling transitioners, it's likely that it hasn't), parents find themselves drifting into the third stage of parenting:

consultation/dialogue. When adolescents successfully manage the transition into emerging adulthood, parents remain parents, but they exert their influence in a manner congruent with the boundaries of a newly minted adult-to-adult relationship. Like consultants in the business world, parents have plenty of wisdom, advice, and guidance to offer, but they concede that the issues at hand are more the transitioner's business than their own—for example, which courses to select, what job to take, whom to date, where to live, and so on.

That's the natural history of parenting in a nutshell. As the management of tasks and responsibilities migrates inexorably across the relationship boundary from parent to child, the parents' primary focus evolves from supervision/caretaking to negotiation and accountability and finally to consultation/dialogue. Each of these stages involves a different paradigm—a sort of contract—for managing the parent-child relationship. This paradigm, or contract, is composed of unspoken, largely unconscious assumptions and ground rules about the relational boundaries—the question of whose business is what. When a young child makes poor choices or behaves impulsively, it is ultimately the parents who own the responsibility for getting the child back on course. No one has to say that out loud or even to consciously formulate it. It's just the way things are. It's the proper paradigm, or contract, of parenting a young child.

In adolescence, the paradigm changes, again without any conscious deliberation. Adolescents likewise may make poor choices or behave impulsively, and they bear some of the responsibility for their behavior. But parents still share in this responsibility, and the contract requires parents to do whatever they can to find ways of solving the adolescent's problems. If your sixteen-year-old is skipping school, using drugs, or treating family members poorly, you may not have the power to change this behavior, but you nevertheless have an obligation to try. That's the contract. You can't tell them they'll have to move out, and you can't refuse essential material support just because they are uncooperative and troublesome. Those options are not in the contract. When you are the parent of a troublesome adolescent, you are stuck with him or her—period! And the paradigm works both ways. If you're the troublesome adolescent, you know deep down that this is the contract—that your parents are committed, for better or for worse.

This is precisely the problem for Nick and his parents. They are unconsciously trapped in the relational paradigm of adolescence. Nick continues to think and react like an adolescent because the assumptions and ground rules that underlie and organize their relationship allow him to do so. No one intends this, not even Nick. The underlying relational paradigm is more powerful than the individual family members themselves, and in Nick's case, it has all three trapped in an adolescent time warp. Seth and Renée tell Nick that civil behavior is a *requirement* of his continuing to live at home, but in fact it's more of a *recommendation*. The only true requirement for Nick living at home and receiving his parents' continued support is the one stipulated in the contract of the adolescent-parent relationship: namely, that he is their son.

For Seth and Renée to help Nick find his way to adulthood,

they will have to change the underlying assumptions and ground rules of their relationship. They're going to have to shift gears from the supervision and negotiation stages of parenting and redefine themselves in terms of the consultation/dialogue stage—a process that starts with a clarification of the boundaries appropriate to that developmental stage. In short, they must together sort out what properly is their business and what is Nick's.

Fix the Boundaries, Not the Behavior

When I first brought up the goal of changing their parenting paradigm, Seth and Renée seemed to understand the concept but had difficulty identifying how this would work in real life. As a family therapist, I spent years learning how to identify and evaluate relational boundaries. So it comes as no surprise to me that most people, even if they understand the concept of boundaries, have difficulty assessing them as a concrete reality in their own relationships. Relational boundaries are invisible. We *feel* them more than we can definitively identify and describe them.

Whenever I work with parents who find it difficult to envision what a more adult-to-adult, parent-as-consultant relationship with their struggling transitioner might look like, I give them what I call the distant nephew (or niece) thought experiment. This helps them to envision the developmental goal of their parenting. I asked Seth and Renée to imagine how they would behave differently if Nick was not their son but instead was a distant nephew who had come from far away to live with them. It's easier to sort out whose business is what when you're talking about someone else's child, rather than your own sons and daughters.

My wife and I learned this principle through a real-life experiment. The year following our daughter's graduation from high school and beginning college—our first year as empty nesters—I was contacted by a private school where I consult and asked if I would consider taking on a boarder. A young woman whose family had moved to another city wanted to return to the school for her senior year. I was ambivalent, as I had briefly counseled this young woman during her previous tenure at the school and knew that she was no angel. We had more than a few misgivings about what we might be getting ourselves into. Nevertheless, after much discussion, we agreed to take her in.

It turned out to be the easiest year of "parenting" we ever had—by far—and our own two kids hadn't been all that challenging, so that's saying something. For example, our new boarder, our "distant niece," smoked cigarettes. But the boundaries around this particular issue, just like all the other issues we faced that year, were uncommonly clear. Her lungs and her long-term health were her business, not ours. But her third-floor bedroom and the rest of the house, including the garden beneath her bedroom window, where cigarette butts could easily accumulate—these were our business, plain and simple. This clear boundary allowed us to take a completely hands-off attitude toward her smoking, but at the same time, an uncompromising, nonnegotiable position regarding smoking inside the house. But the real story is that these clear boundaries enabled us to have a wonderful, friendly, conflict-free relationship with her for the entire school year.

Of course, our own sons and daughters are not just boarders, nor are they distant nephews and nieces. We care too much to regard them in the same way, which is why boundaries get tangled in the first place. But if you're committed to helping your struggling transitioner make better decisions, untangling the boundaries of your relationship is the most effective way to do it. The distant nephew thought experiment is just a tool for helping you to envision the sort of adult-to-adult boundaries and parent-as-consultant role that you need to shoot for.

I walked Seth and Renée through the thought experiment with a series of leading questions. The conversation went something like this.

"If Nick was your nephew instead of your son, would you be working so hard to get his life on track?" I asked.

"Well, we'd certainly offer our help, but only if he seemed interested and receptive."

"What about school?" I continued.

"Same thing," they answered. "We'd be more than happy to help him out. Young people need guidance. But we wouldn't impose our ideas on him."

"What about his drinking?"

"Well, we'd be concerned about that and would probably share our concerns, but the bottom line would be that we would not put up with his coming home intoxicated and waking us up. And we'd probably have a house curfew, just for our own peace of mind."

"What about his behavior around the house and his habit of taking your beers and 'borrowing' your lighter?" I prodded.

"Well, that would be out of the question," they stated flatly. "We'd tell him that civil behavior and respect for our property was a house rule, a nonnegotiable."

"And if he chose to ignore your house rules?" I continued.

"Well then, he'd have to leave," they hesitantly concluded.

"You mean, you'd just THROW HIM OUT INTO THE STREET?" I asked dramatically.

"No, no, we wouldn't throw him out. But we'd explain that it just wasn't working for us and that he'd have to find another place to stay. And then we'd probably help him with that, finding an apartment or a rental or whatever, provided he was open to our help. If he was our nephew, then he's family, and we wouldn't want to end the relationship. We'd just want to get him out from under our roof."

This was, of course, just a thought experiment, and thought experiments are simple. But it helped Seth and Renée create a picture in their minds of what clearer boundaries might look like in their relationship with Nick. It gave them a starting point—a plan—with which to begin rethinking their relationship with Nick.

What Nick's Parents Did

Nick's parents made two important changes in their parenting paradigm. Using the distant nephew principle as a guideline, they informed Nick that they were going to drop their various efforts to steer him toward a better-paying job and a return to school. They made it clear that they were available to consult with him on these matters, but that their input would come only at his request. In other words, they formally declared Nick's business to be just that—Nick's business.

The other thing they did—and equally important—was to spell out definitively what they considered to be *their* business, which included room, board, house rules, and ongoing financial support. They sat down with Nick and presented him with two options: He could decide to live by house rules, or they could all get together, in a spirit of optimism and support, and help him find an alternative to living at home. Of course the three had "discussed" the possibility of his living elsewhere numerous times, but always in a mode of conflict—arguing, threatening, and so on. This time the conversation was different. Instead of Mom and Dad threatening, "If you can't shape up, you'll have to leave," and Nick counter-threatening to "just leave if you don't get off my back," they discussed moving out as a positive possibility. They considered whether it might help Nick feel better about himself and if it might improve their relationship. They framed this possibility as a win-win arrangement. They informed him that in the event he did decide to move out, they would provide a time-limited "rent subsidy" equal to their approximate expense for having him at home.

At the same time they raised the possibility of Nick's moving out, they also spelled out the alternative option of continuing to live at home. And while they had raised this issue many times before—always with an air of exasperation—this conversation likewise had a very different tone. Most important, they made clear that their house rules, which they presented matter-of-factly as nonnegotiable (pick up after yourself, keep decent hours, behave in a civil fashion, etc.), had nothing to do with trying to shape up Nick. They weren't meant as implied criticism or discipline, but were simply a practical matter of making their *own* day-to-day lives smoother and more comfortable.

"These are things *we* need in order to be comfortable having you under our roof," they explained. On the surface, Nick and his parents had tried versions of this conversation many times before. But this time was decidedly different. Now the discussion was organized around a different set of boundaries—a clear demarcation of Nick's business, his parents' business, and their shared business. Different boundaries = different conversations = different outcomes—it's that simple.

■ ■ ■

We all know, however, that in real life, growth and change is never simple. Several weeks went by with little further conversation about the matter of living at home or moving out, though Nick's behavior became noticeably more subdued and civil. Something had changed, and Nick knew it. His parents' proposal was a first step toward untangling the adolescent dynamics of their relationship, effectively shifting the dilemma of managing Nick's living situation and his household behavior from their side of the boundary to his.

In my biweekly therapy sessions with Nick, I saw the change immediately. Initially he was excited about the option of moving out, speculating on how great it would be. But his excitement quickly abated as we explored the nuts and bolts of moving out and taking on more responsibility for supporting himself. I put Nick in touch with a friend who owned several houses that he rented to college students near a local campus so Nick could find roommates. This contact led to a new line of thinking and discussion in our sessions.

"What's a security deposit?" he wanted to know. "How much do utilities cost? What happens if I don't get along with my housemates?" Nick's steady mantra of parental complaints was replaced with these and similar real-world questions—questions that touched on the concrete problems and dilemmas of independent living. With these questions came a slowly dawning, uncomfortable realization of what his parents had known all along—namely, that independent living was probably beyond Nick's current means, even with his parents proposed (but limited) rent subsidy. Buying groceries, keeping up his car payment, and paying for cell phone service: Nick did the math, and the math didn't add up. Nick briefly considered a more affordable third-floor room with empty nesters in his neighborhood, but when I pointed out that they would likely have house rules similar to those of his parents, Nick lost interest and resigned himself to the inevitable.

At this point in our counseling, Nick's demeanor changed dramatically. He became more subdued, a bit confused, and noticeably more anxious. Nick was beginning to feel the effects of *ownership* of the developmental challenges he had avoided all this time. Nick had been much more comfortable with the familiar adolescent-parent relationship, in which his parents both supported and nagged, while he righteously complained about their efforts to micromanage him. It was only a matter of time before Nick came to the conclusion that, for the time being at least, he needed to stay at home, and that keeping house rules was a reasonable price to keep this option open.

I continued to work with Nick, and occasionally his parents, for another six months. During that time, Nick set his immediate sights on earning and saving enough money to be able to move into his own place. He pushed harder for increased hours at his job and submitted applications to a number of similar businesses in the area, eventually landing a position that paid better and offered more hours. For the first time, Nick had a goal that mattered to him—and that focused his energies. His story, as far as I was a part of it, had a decidedly positive outcome, and one that was somewhat unexpected. Around the time that moving out became a realistic possibility—Nick was now making more money and had saved several thousand dollars—he started contemplating a return to school. "This working thing is hard," he announced to me one day. Nick had begun to see the handwriting on the wall—namely, that he was on a track that led to a modest lifestyle and inevitable frustrations. School began to make sense, no longer as a way to *avoid* growing up, as it had been on his first go-round, but as a way of making growing up easier in the long run. When I last saw Nick, he was about to enroll as a full-time student at a local community college, with a plan to transfer to a four-year school once he reestablished his academic bona fides.

Parents should know:

One important goal of counseling with a struggling transitioner is just this: getting my client to begin worrying about the right things—the things that make growing up happen over time. Experience has taught me, time and again, that counseling a struggling transitioner is nearly impossible as long as they remain mired in the tangled dance of adolescent family dynamics. When parents take definitive steps to clarify and redefine those boundaries, as Nick's parents did, my job gets easier. In a matter of a month or so, Nick transformed from a twenty-two-year-old-going-on-sixteen to a twenty-two-year-old-going-on-twenty-five, worrying about the right things, asking the right questions, and confronting the dilemmas and challenges of becoming an adult.

If you have a twentysomething in your life who resembles Nick or Kyle or Bridie or any of the struggling transitioners who have surfaced in these pages, I want you to know there's hope! The challenging part lies in shifting away from the "common sense" (but counterproductive) approach of attempting to directly intervene to redirect their behavior—the missteps and the omissions, the foot-dragging and poor decisions—the way you would (quite appropriately) with a child or adolescent. Stop crossing your fingers; your son or daughter isn't going to wake up tomorrow suddenly behaving like an adult. But there's no reason *you* can't wake up tomorrow with a different vision of your relationship, and a different game plan for your parenting.

- Think about the *underlying relational paradigm* of your relationship and try to identify all the ways it feels more adolescent than adult.
- Look for the tangled boundaries I described throughout this chapter. Are there ways you can start to move from a supervisory/caretaking or negotiation and accountability sort of relationship with your transitioner to one defined by consultation and dialogue?
- Try the distant nephew/niece thought experiment I used with Seth and Renée to help you see new possibilities. And then instead of obsessively focusing on your transitioner's immature and errant behavior, focus on the way you think about your job description for parenting a twentysomething.

Goodbye, parent supervisor. Hello, parent consultant. A new day is dawning!

Chapter 9

The Mystery of Motivation

Creating Necessity for Your
Struggling Transitioner

Twenty-year-old Jake and his father, Frank, are a perfect example of how motivational issues can become the centerpiece of the interaction between parent and transitioner. Jake had been a poor student in high school, and after a year of community college decided that advanced education wasn't for him. For the next year, before I came into the picture, he continued to live at home, working various part-time jobs. The majority of his time and energy was invested in his girlfriend, and despite talking a good game about finding serious work, he hadn't done much to make it happen. Jake was a good kid, not getting into any significant trouble, not drinking to excess or using drugs, but also not doing much to move himself along the developmental curve toward self-sufficiency.

Jake's dad had secured a warehouse job for him some months before we first met, but Jake had quit after several weeks, complaining that the work was unbearably boring and the people he worked with were "not his type." He wanted work that was "interesting" and "meaningful" and wasn't going to waste time in a dead-end job. Like many transitioners entering the adult workforce, Jake was paralyzed by the fact that attractive entry-level jobs, particularly for those without advanced education, are few and far between. For transitioners like Jake, it's not necessarily that they're without interests and goals (I've had struggling clients who wanted to become novelists, screenwriters, video game designers, FBI agents, and a host of other occupations); it's that they can't imagine or accept the pedestrian beginnings that might lead to these destinations. The result, as we saw with Andrew back in chapter 6—and here with Jake—is that they become stalled and discouraged, perpetuating the holding pattern of prolonged adolescence.

One of the most common complaints I hear from parents is that their struggling transitioners lack the motivation to do what they need to do. This was the case for Nick's parents in the last chapter, and for the parents of almost every client mentioned in this book. Each of these parents came to me with variations of this central dilemma: "How do I *get* my son/daughter to . . . apply for a job . . . sign up for classes . . . just get out of bed in the morning?"

Jake's dad, Frank, did what parents of struggling transitioners usually do: He tried to *motivate* Jake. He gave him encouragement, he tried to be emotionally supportive, he brainstormed job and occupational possibilities, and he held forth on the importance of initiative, goals, "taking the bull by the horns," and the virtues of self-reliance. He got angry with Jake, he threatened to withhold support, he offered incentives, and he set deadlines.

He did everything he could, in his words, "to stir some fire in the belly," but to no avail. "Honestly," he confided to me, "I feel like I could get a second career as a motivational speaker!"

How Do You *Get* Someone to Do Something?

Motivation is one of the great mysteries of human behavior, so it's worth our while to learn some of what social scientists know about it. Research offers two models of how motivation works. There's *extrinsic* motivation, which derives from the environment, usually in the form of rewards, punishments, consequences, or threats. Then there's *intrinsic* motivation, which bubbles up within the individual, usually in the form of interest, initiative, and in the best of all possible scenarios, passion. Daniel Pink, who has written compellingly on the subject of human motivation, notes that intrinsic motivation is a far more effective driver of learning and behavior change than extrinsic motivation. Extrinsic motivators (rewards and punishments)—as well as they might work with animals, small children, and occasionally adolescents—are notoriously ineffective with emerging adults. In fact, research shows that extrinsic motivators actually have a long-term effect of *diminishing* intrinsic motivation, which is the last thing we want to accomplish with the Jakes and Nicks of the world.

These facts lead directly to the heart of our motivational

catch-22: How can a parent (by definition an extrinsic motiva-tional source) influence the emergence of intrinsic motivation? This was precisely the intent of Frank's "fire in the belly" speech, and we saw that his efforts led nowhere. This intrinsic-extrinsic conundrum sounds like an unsolvable riddle—but it really isn't.

If Frank is going to "get" Jake motivated to start looking for a job, he's going to have to try a different approach. The problem with Frank's current strategy is embedded in his question: "How do I *get* Jake to start looking for a real job?" The fact that Frank is trying to *get* Jake to do something implies that this something—in this case, looking for a job—is *Frank's* agenda, not Jake's. In other words, Frank and Jake are caught in the same boundary tangle we saw in the previous chapter. Frank has made Jake's business *his* business, and Jake is having none of it. Resolving the mystery of motivation, it turns out, is an-other (somewhat more complicated) instance of sorting out whose business is what.

Creative Adjustment

Frank, like so many frustrated parents of struggling transition-ers, was operating implicitly under the model of intrinsic moti-vation. He committed to the impossible task of stirring up initiative and interest on Jake's side of the relationship. My job was to introduce Frank to a new model of motivation, one known as *creative adjustment*. In the creative adjustment model, motiva-tion and learning derive neither solely from the individual (intrinsic motivation) nor solely from the environment (extrinsic motivation). Instead, it derives from a meeting of the two.

Creative adjustment refers to the adaptations we make when we are confronted with circumstances presenting the twin conditions of *challenge* and *necessity*. Challenge in this context means that the task at hand lays beyond our *currently* established repertoire of competence and mastery. It lays at the growing edge of our development, something we are capable of but which also has a quality of novelty—a new problem to be solved. It may be as simple as learning how to write a check or fill out a job application, or as complex as learning to operate a manual transmission or preparing one's income taxes for the first time.

The quality of necessity means that the situation *requires* that we deal with the challenge at hand. It's not something we can afford to put aside or avoid. For example, do you know how to change a tire? If the answer is yes, chances are pretty high that at some point you were confronted with the *necessity* of *adjusting creatively* to the *challenging situation* of a flat tire. You probably got out the owner's manual, found the jack and spare tire stored in the trunk of your car, and either followed the instructions or figured it out yourself. Most of us were not *intrinsically* motivated to go out to the garage one sunny afternoon and teach ourselves the process of changing the tire just for future reference. More likely, we found ourselves by the side of the road with somewhere to go, challenged by a flat tire that wasn't going to fix itself.

The acquisition of these skills, simple and complex, and the accrual of confidence that comes with their mastery are what we call creative adjustment. Whereas intrinsic interest and passion may be what gives our lives a sense of joy and purpose, and extrinsic rewards and consequences may have helped us attain specific goals, it's creative adjustment that did most of the work of carrying us from each developmental stage to the next. It's the nuts and bolts of growing up. And the reason this concept is so important to parenting is that while Frank may have been powerless to get Jake motivated, he *was* capable of creating conditions of challenge and necessity that could help Jake to motivate himself.

The Magic of Challenge and Necessity

Some years ago, a young client taught me the critical importance of challenge and necessity for struggling transitioners; I'll call him Rhett. Rhett, at twenty-one, had had a tough go at it, accumulating enough difficult life experience to render him grizzled and wise and wary. At the time he came to see me, he was, he announced, ready to grow up, but he also had zero confidence that he could survive out there in the "real world." Here's his story:

Rhett's parents divorced when he was just a little boy, and his mother was awarded sole custody, as his father's work took him all over the country. His mom was a sincere and well-intending parent, but no match for an energetic boy with a penchant for pushing limits and seeking excitement. As a teenager, he pretty much blew off school and plunged headlong into the street and drug culture of his working-class neighborhood. By age sixteen, he was dealing drugs, mostly selling marijuana to classmates, and probably making more money than his mother, who was completely overmatched in her various efforts to rein him in and get him on the straight and narrow. She appealed to his mostly absent but very successful father, who intervened by having Rhett placed in a wilderness therapeutic program in the western part of the country. Rhett went kicking and screaming, literally, but returned home six months later (three in the wilderness program, and three in a therapeutic boarding school), a more settled, relational, and goal-oriented kid. He began his senior year at his old high school with good intentions, but within several months had relapsed, both in terms of his drug involvement and his outlaw lifestyle. His parents joined forces quickly and had him "escorted," once again, to a restrictive therapeutic setting. This time, however, his letters home displayed none of the self-examining reflection and regret that his previous experience had yielded. He was angry, and upon turning eighteen, left the program abruptly, returned home, and settled into an apartment with several of his old street pals. In fact, he would have nothing to do with his parents, accusing them of ruining his life. He could make it on his own, he declared defiantly.

Except, it turned out, he couldn't. Several months later, Rhett was back to his old line of work, selling mostly pot and, occasionally, opioid pills. He refused contact with either of his parents, other than to to let them know every once in a while that he was doing fine on his own and did not need their support.

Until he did. Rhett had the bad (though actually good) fortune of selling some pills to an undercover detective, and Rhett's high-flying enterprise and newfound independence came crashing to a halt. He was busted, big time.

Rhett was, as the saying goes, up shit's creek, and he was given a choice: He could go to trial and quite possibly face some months of prison time, or he could roll up on the dealer he hustled for. If he chose the latter, he would receive a suspended sentence—with an additional stipulation of undergoing drug rehab and straightening out his life (i.e., reconnecting with his family and getting himself some therapy).

This was indeed what Rhett wisely chose to do: He entered a local rehab program and came to the painful realization that he had been fooling himself with his faux independence. He took to rehab seriously, moved back in with his mom, and regularly attended AA and NA meetings.

This entire history unfolded a good year before I was introduced to Rhett. When I met him, his sobriety and newfound humility and civility were real, if unsteady. The bluster of adolescence was gone, replaced by the anxiety and uncertainty of his nascent transition toward adulthood. The problem was that Rhett could not get himself in gear to enter the "real world" of grown-up society, either educationally or in the workforce. He stated that his energies were absorbed in his efforts to protect and maintain his precarious sobriety and good citizenship, which involved meetings pretty much every day or evening. He was afraid what would happen once he left the protective bubble of his mom's benevolent oversight and his twelve-step program. Would he meet the wrong people, encounter old associates, break down under the weight of real-world pressures and expectations? His parents, likewise protective, were reluctant to apply pressure on Rhett to find employment or return to school. And to be truthful, I myself, in light of the chaotic and perilous history they detailed when first I met them, was anxious lest I push him past the limits of his tenuous and tentative transition from rebellious, outlaw adolescence toward responsible emerging adulthood.

In therapy, I did my best to help Rhett reframe his narrative about himself—from screw-up and snitch to a lost adolescent who got caught up in something much larger than him (i.e., an epidemic sweeping the country), and who rightly intuited that doing prison time would likely spell the end of any prospects for a future. I framed his considerable anxiety and insecurity as a reasonable response to the formidable challenge of venturing into uncharted territory and making a viable life for himself. I told him things I tell most transitioners his age, like "none of us had it figured out when we were your age," and "you think you're way behind, but most people don't figure out their life until they're around thirty." But words and encouragement can only do so much, and Rhett, despite his good intentions and hopes for the future, remained housebound in an almost agoraphobic-like way. Despite my best efforts, I was unable to generate a beckoning future self, a sense of direction and purpose that would break the spell of his inertia.

Then Rhett, reasoning that he would be more comfortable in his housebound state if he had a companion, adopted a dog from an animal rescue shelter. The dog he adopted—and here's where fate got involved—was a mix with a large component of Labrador retriever. Labrador retrievers, it turns out, require a great deal of exercise—a seemingly minor detail with important un-foreseen consequences.

His dog shared none of the apprehension and hesitation evinced by Rhett, his parents, and his therapist. Rhett reflected later: "It was the first time in my life that I didn't really feel I had any choice in the matter. He had to be fed, he had to be run—and boy, did he run! He needed my attention. And he didn't hesitate to let me know when I was falling down on the job!" It was the first time Rhett could recall subordinating his own needs and impulses to the needs and requirements of something beyond himself. He settled into a daily routine of managing these re-sponsibilities, and—not surprising—began incrementally to feel better about himself. Rhett's Lab provided him with the chal-lenge and necessity that was otherwise missing in his life. He left the house several times daily, and searched the surrounding farm and parkland to identify the best trails for his dog to express his Labradorian essence. He found a local dog park where they both made friends, and where Rhett could practice the rudi-ments of ordinary conversation with other dog owners.

In therapy, Rhett's energy level and confidence showed a pro-nounced uptick, and in a matter of a few weeks he proudly announced that he was beginning to volunteer at the animal shelter. In several months, this evolved into a paid staff-level po-sition at the shelter. Rhett, and his dog, were on their way.

These events occurred several years back. Some months ago, I contacted Rhett and asked if I could interview him for this book. Was he still at the shelter? I asked. "No," he replied. He was just then finishing up automotive repair training at a regional vocational school. His dad was a very successful mechanical engineer, and Rhett, drawing from the same gene pool, had found a way to harness his natural talents into a career on which he could build a life. "Give that pup a treat for me," I said as Rhett left the coffee shop where we met. Big broad smile: "You bet!" answered Rhett.

The true hero of Rhett's story was, of course, his dog, who provided the magic ingredients that neither his parents—nor his therapist—could engineer: challenge and necessity.

"Getting It"

A better question for Frank to ask with respect to Jake's lack of motivation was this: "What conditions or circumstances would facilitate Jake *getting it*—that he needs to get serious about finding full-time work?" Whereas the "getting" of Frank's initial question lay on *his* side of the boundary, the "getting" of *getting it* lay on Jake's side. And unlike Frank's initial question, this one had an answer.

What does *getting it* mean? In psychological research, *getting it* falls under the heading of what psychologists have long called insight learning. Insight learning is different from habit acquisition or skill development—forms of learning that require repetition and the gradual building of a particular behavior pattern. Insight learning refers to situations in which a learner connects the dots and comes to understand—often in an *aha!* moment—how the diverse elements of a challenging situation fit together. The learner begins to see a pattern and then alters his or her behavior on the basis of the new insight. This is exactly what you're trying to get your undermotivated, struggling transitioner to do—connect the dots and *get it* that he or she has to change his or her ways and take initiative. But how can parents help to make this happen?

The experimental model for insight learning was developed almost a century ago, by a psychologist named Wolfgang Köhler. Knowing that apes were among the smartest creatures in the animal kingdom, Köhler devised a series of experiments to demonstrate their capacity for higher forms of learning. In one experiment, he placed bananas outside the cage (and just out of reach) of a bright ape named Sultan. When positioning the food, Köhler used a small rake to move it around. He then leaned the rake against the side of Sultan's cage, and let the situation unfold. After trying repeatedly—and unsuccessfully—to reach the bananas with his hands, Sultan sat down and contemplated his perplexing situation. He was hungry and food was in sight, but he couldn't get it. Köhler described what happened next. Sultan looked back and forth from the rake to the food for some time. Back and forth, back and forth . . . And then, in an instant of insight, Sultan grabbed the rake, extended it through the bars of his cage, and pulled the food within reach.

Voilà! Lunch for Sultan.

I am not comparing your struggling transitioner to Köhler's ape. The comparison is instead one between you, the parent of an unmotivated struggling transitioner, and Köhler himself. You are faced with the same challenge. How do you *get* someone (or some ape) to do something you want them to do? Köhler's experiment helps us to understand the shift in perspective that I'm proposing. Köhler's question might be formulated thus: What are the *conditions* that would support Sultan in *getting it*, that is to say, making the connection between the elements of the situation—his hunger, the frustrating limitations of the cage, the rake, and the food?

Asking the question "What are the *conditions* that create motivation and learning?"—instead of "How do I *motivate* another person?"—makes all the difference in the world.

What Are the Conditions that Activate Motivation?

Köhler's ingenious experiment gives us the answer. He provided Sultan with *challenge* (the problem of getting the bananas) and *necessity* (depriving him of food, so as to generate his hunger).

This is a critical part of the formula in motivating your struggling transitioner: First, accept the paradoxical starting point that you can't *get* them to do what you wish they would be doing, at least not directly. Second, begin strategizing about challenge and necessity. If you're frustrated by an unmotivated transitioner, it may be that you are unintentionally short-circuiting the challenge and necessity that your transitioner so desperately needs to grow up. There's also a third element to the motivational formula: *support*. Sultan couldn't have solved his problem if Köhler hadn't helped by providing the rake and modeling its use. Of course, support for struggling transitioners is much trickier than simply supplying tools and modeling. In fact, support has such a crucial and complex impact on transitioner motivation that it will be addressed in both chapters 10 and 11.

Creating supportive conditions of challenge and necessity, as Köhler did with Sultan, was actually an ingenious roundabout way of generating *intrinsic* motivation. What Köhler did, in essence, was to create a *puzzle* for Sultan to solve. Animal behavior researchers have shown that primates are intrinsically drawn toward puzzles and find solving them to be its own reward. Your task as the parent of an unmotivated transitioner is analogous. You've got to figure out a way to follow Köhler's blueprint in creating a solvable puzzle.

Here's how that worked out with Frank and Jake.

I convinced Frank to ditch his fruitless efforts to motivate Jake to begin looking for a serious job—and to begin thinking instead about how he might leave the bananas just far enough outside the cage that Jake would begin problem-solving on his own.

"Does Jake have any bills?" I asked.

"Bills?" Frank replied. "How's he going to manage any bills until he has an income?"

"Actually," I responded, "it usually works the other way around. Kids like Jake need bills in order for the light to come on about working. Right now work is a luxury in Jake's mind. With a few bills, it will become a necessity."

"Well," Frank replied, "he does have a car payment, but he's not making it."

"How's the car payment set up?" I inquired. Here's where the tangled boundaries from the previous chapter came into play.

The car payment was $600 a month; Jake's obligation was to pay his dad $300, while his dad made up the difference. But Jake wasn't holding up his end of the deal, leaving his dad in the classic transitioner parenting dilemma—either making the entire payment himself or getting rid of the car. Frank could have let the bank repossess the car, but his signature was on the loan, and he wasn't about to damage his own credit rating to make a point. He could have sold the car, but he reasoned that transportation was indispensable for Jake to hold down a job. Frank felt trapped in an insoluble catch-22.

I suggested a different approach, one that would sort out the tangled boundary and put the business of the car on a more adult-to-adult footing. The confused boundary wasn't really about the money; it was about ownership of the *necessity*. The problem was that Frank cared more about the financing of Jake's car than Jake did. In other words, the problem was on the wrong side of the parent-child boundary, and Frank's challenge was to transfer it from his shoulders onto Jake's.

Here's what I advised. "Instead of Jake paying or not paying you the $300, and you paying the finance company, why not set it up the other way around? Give Jake the monthly payment coupon book, write him a monthly check for your portion of the payment, and let him manage the mechanics of making the payment. Let him wrestle with the challenge of keeping the car from being repossessed, rather than you."

This is exactly what Frank did. Predictably, as the end of the first month approached, Jake came to his dad and asked if he could "borrow" $150 to make the car payment. Frank loved telling this part of the story. "I smiled sympathetically and turned my pockets inside out." Within days, Jake was looking for a serious job.

This is what Seth and Renée did with Nick in the previous chapter. They rewrote the menu of options open to Nick concerning his living arrangements. He could move out (with their support), or he could accept and abide by their reasonable house rules. This change of paradigm relocated the need for problem-solving from their side of the boundary to Nick's, creating a circumstance of challenge and necessity. Like Köhler's Sultan, Nick wrestled with the problem, and with my support arrived at a paradigm-changing insight: If he wished to continue with viable and comfortable living conditions, he was going to have to change his outlook and his behavior.

The mystery of motivation, it turns out, is just another variation of the boundary confusion that typifies the relationships of parents and their struggling transitioners. When the experience of necessity lies on the parental side of the relational boundary, we find parents like Frank working hard to "get" their transitioner to do what they need to do. When necessity is relocated to the transitioner side of the boundary, transitioners are much more likely to "get it"—i.e., understand that something needs to change.

When Being Unmotivated Isn't About Motivation

What allowed Nick and Jake to respond constructively to the conditions of challenge and necessity their parents arranged is that they were both *capable* of what their parents were requiring them to do. Keep in mind that this isn't always the case. If, for example, your transitioner is suffering from a clinical depression that robs him of energy and optimism or an anxiety disorder that overwhelms her with dread and panic or a chemical dependency that impairs his capacity for rational thought and behavior, then all the motivational strategy in the world isn't going to help. A mental health professional trained in clinical diagnosis and familiar with the developmental challenges of emerging adulthood can sort out the clinical from the situational dimensions of an apparent lack of motivation. If you think clinical impairment is a possibility, I strongly suggest you schedule a joint consultation with a qualified professional for you and your transitioner. If you believe your struggling transitioner's impairment is beyond your capabilities to influence, I want you to read the appendix ("Getting Professional Help"), where I'll address this situation. I'll walk you through some of the options available for getting you the support you need and coach you on how to effectively approach mental health resources and practitioners. Don't give up! There are plenty of committed and competent professionals who are experts at the emerging adulthood transition.

Parents should know:

- Your job is *not* to motivate your struggling transitioner. Instead, it's to create the circumstances that support motivation. Remember, you're not supervising or negotiating anymore! You're moving toward a consultation role in this relationship.

- Look for opportunities that promote creative adjustment and create the necessity for transitioners to change on their own.

Chapter 10

Breaking the Enabling Trap

Supporting (Not Coddling)
Your Struggling Transitioner

A common denominator for virtually all the struggling transitioners we've met in these pages is that they take their parents' material and financial support for granted. In fact, most of the transitioners I see in therapy or whose parents I see in consultation display a striking naiveté concerning the nitty-gritty of financial reality. We saw this with Jake, who treated his car as an entitlement, rather than an obligation. We saw this with Nick in chapters 1 and 8, who regarded his parents' home and possessions as his own. Gordon from chapter 7 seemed to think college was some sort of extended vacation, and treated the apartment his parents so generously provided like a fraternity house. It seems that financial immaturity is virtually a trademark of struggling transitioners—a kind of obliviousness to the reality of what things cost and the obligations that go with being funded by one's parents. "She or he takes our support for granted" is among the most common complaints I hear from parents of struggling transitioners.

This chapter tackles three important questions: Why do kids think this way? How do parents contribute to the problem? And finally, what can parents do about it?

Why Transitioners Take Material Support for Granted

I began to answer this question with the help of a twenty-one-year-old client named Kaylee, who had a lot of trouble with money. Like many incoming college students, she acquired her first credit card during first-year orientation, when banks set up booths on campus and solicit applications for new accounts. And like many transitioners with their first credit cards, she maxed out her credit limit within months, requiring a parental bailout to restore solvency.

Lesson learned, right? Wrong. Kaylee did exactly the same thing during her second year of college, necessitating a second bailout, a stern lecture, and a mandatory tutorial with her father on the utilization of spreadsheets and the art of budgeting.

In her third year of college, Kaylee was on a short financial leash, with her dad sharing her bank and credit card accounts to monitor her spending. Kaylee stayed within her budget, more or less, for the better part of the school year—until spring break. On a road trip with roommates to New York City, she racked up several thousand dollars in charges, which brought me into the picture. Home for the summer, and with her parents convinced that something was seriously wrong, Kaylee was required to attend therapy.

Kaylee found it difficult to discuss her strange spending behavior, which she herself recognized as irrational and irresponsible. She would start a sentence with something like "I don't know, I just . . ." and then trail off into embarrassed silence. I looked for all the usual suspects. Was she trying to impress her friends? Was she angry with her parents? Had she felt shortchanged by her parents compared to a favored sibling? Kaylee was open to exploring all of these possibilities, but none of them resonated emotionally or triggered any insight into her impulsive spending behavior.

It's legitimate to be concerned about behavior that seems so irresponsible. But Kaylee met most of the important benchmarks for emerging adult development. She was a good, responsible student; she did not abuse drugs or alcohol; she held a position of administrative responsibility in a campus organization; and she related to her parents in a manner that seemed— on the surface, at least—more adult than adolescent. It was only her immaturity about money that seemed out of step with the rest of her development.

How can we understand such perplexing behavior?

The Money Tree

At an intellectual level, Kaylee understood a good deal about money. She had taken a high school economics course; she knew what her college tuition cost; she knew the prices of clothing, electronic devices, and concert tickets. She knew that when she went out to dinner with her parents, the bill sometimes reached a hundred dollars. But what she didn't know—because she didn't have to manage the family finances herself—was whether a hundred dollars was a little or a lot. In other words, while she had an abstract understanding of money, she was unable to translate that hundred-dollar restaurant bill into quantities of effort, obligation, or worry, the way most adults can in a flash.

Kaylee turned out to be another one of my "poets"—she managed to express something eloquently in therapy that is true for many clients but that most are unable to put into words. Here's what Kaylee told me: "When I was a little girl, my parents used to joke about their 'money tree.' And I just got this picture in my head—that they would go somewhere and pick money off a tree. I knew it wasn't actually true, but it *felt* true, and the picture has just stayed with me. Rationally I know it's ridiculous, but it's still the image that flashes through my mind whenever I ask for something that costs money."

Kaylee and her money tree were a lot like my daughter and the family cars. She was putting something into words that felt true because metaphorically it *was* true. Her parents had provided for her throughout her childhood and adolescence and were continuing to do so in her transitioning years. And because this financial safety net—this money tree—had always been there, she was afforded the luxury of taking it for granted.

This idea is frequently difficult for parents to grasp, because they naturally think of money as an objective reality. They think of the math, rather than the subjective *meaning* that defines money for their transitioner. I often ask parents the following question when they scratch their heads about this: "When is the last time you stopped to appreciate the wonderful interstate highway system we have in the United States?" They usually look at me as if I'm crazy to ask such an irrelevant question. But then I say, "If you had recently traveled to a developing country, you'd be celebrating how easy it is for us to get from one city to the next. If you haven't had that experience recently, you take it for granted, because it's always been here."

That's very much the way it is for our children when it comes to the cost of a smartphone or internet service, to say nothing of the cost of an education and the roof over their heads. And when we come up against this absence of awareness and appreciation, we are befuddled; and yes (to quote my daughter), we act like we own the cars!

The Role of Shame

Naiveté isn't the complete answer for why many struggling transitioners take their parents' financial and material support for granted. It's also that if you're a twentysomething, financially dependent upon your parents and not adequately preparing for financial independence, you likely don't *want* to become fully aware of your situation. Many transitioners I work with eventually acknowledge a deep sense of shame over their lack of progress compared to more successful peers and former classmates. Theirs is a purposeful obliviousness; it's simply more comfortable to continue thinking like an adolescent. It saves face by avoiding what would otherwise be a painful acknowledgment of an underlying sense of failure and inadequacy. Twenty-four-year-old Ricky was a perfect case in point. After completing two years in the armed services, during which he was trained in medical equipment repair, he was smart and employable, but he was hindered by a know-it-all attitude and an inability to acknowledge mistakes. This made it impossible for him to keep a job for more than a few months, and in periods of unemployment, he moved back home with his parents.

His attitude at home was much the same that brought him into conflict with employers. "He acts like we owe him something," his mother lamented in my office. "He acts like he's doing us a favor." Ricky's parents had been clients of mine years before, and when they insisted he meet with a therapist as a condition of remaining at home, he reluctantly came to see me.

I've spent decades working with oppositional defiant adolescents, so I'm familiar with young people like Ricky. I avoid power struggles and defuse their expectations that I'm just a stand-in for Mom and Dad. Toward the end of our initial meeting, during which he had behaved like a hostile witness in a court proceeding, I posed the question "Why are you here?"

"Because my parents made me come," he answered.

"I don't believe it," I countered.

"What do you mean, you don't believe it?"

Shaking my head slowly, I said, almost to myself, "Nope, I just don't buy it."

Confused, he asked, "Why don't you buy it?"

"I don't buy that your parents can make someone do things at your age," I replied. "You're a grown-up."

This exchange was followed by a pause of a minute or so and then Ricky's barely audible reply: "I'm not a grown-up . . . I'm a fuck-up."

There it was. Ricky, a poet in the same sense as Kaylee, was speaking for multitudes of struggling transitioners who are disappointing themselves at least as much as they are disappointing their parents. They keep their deep sense of inadequacy and failure at bay with a variety of psychological defenses—blaming others, avoiding the subject, and good old-fashioned denial, to name a few. They cling to an old paradigm of parent–adolescent relationships in order to avoid the painful acknowledgment of their struggle. And part of this clinging, this avoidance, is that they unconsciously take your continued material support for granted.

The Enabling Trap

Doris was the mother of twenty-one-year-old Jeremy. She contacted me because she was concerned that her son wasn't doing much to prepare himself for adulthood. Her main concern was that Jeremy wasn't in school and was devoting most of his energies to getting a band together. He wasn't having much success, and she wanted to see him support his musical aspirations with college-level training. We talked about how she might pursue the conversation in a fashion that would come across as supportive rather than nagging. She left my office with several concrete ideas about how to approach him, and that was the last I heard from her.

For a while, at least.

Six months later, I received an emergency call from Doris early on a Saturday morning. She told me that her son had recently been doing much better: He was working a part-time job and was enrolled in several college classes. "Why the emergency phone call?" I asked. Doris explained that her son had a terrible driving record and had accumulated three speeding tickets over the previous twelve months. To make matters worse, he had ignored the tickets, neither paying the fines nor responding in any way to the threats and penalties that resulted. That particular morning he had a date in the mayor's traffic court, at which he would be required to pay a hefty sum. Doris called me because he refused to get out of bed—cursing and berating his mother when she tried to rouse him. What should she do? Doris was really concerned.

"Why do anything?" I replied. "Your son is using terrible judgment. But you know the old saying: 'Good judgment comes from wisdom, wisdom comes from making mistakes, and mistakes come from bad judgment.' If you can stand aside, your son will soon enough learn the price of neglecting this responsibility." The matter seemed simple and straightforward to me.

But then again, the conundrums of other people's parenting often seem simple. We hear of someone else's transitioner living on the family dole, messing up in school, avoiding real employment, and generally prolonging an unhealthy adolescent lifestyle. And we say to ourselves, "I would never put up with that!" We really believe it's that simple.

For Doris, however, it wasn't simple at all. "I think he's finally beginning get his act together," she noted. "And if those fines don't get paid this morning, he'll likely lose his driver's license. And that will mean he won't be able to get himself to work—but even worse, he'll have to drop his college classes. He'll be right back where he started—trying to make it with his band, going nowhere. It'll ruin his life!"

Support versus Enabling

Doris found herself ensnared in the enabling trap. Her son wouldn't help himself, and she felt damned if she did and damned if she didn't in saving him from his own bad judgment. You observe your child doing a poor job of managing something that *ought* to be their business—getting a job, signing up for classes, getting out of bed in the morning—and you step forward in an effort to nudge him or her into taking ownership and responsibility for the behavior in question. For many families, this sort of parental nudging is sufficient. He or she takes the hint and gets the haircut for the job interview, begins to make payments on a loan a parent has extended, asks for more hours at work, or helps out around the house. But it's situations like Doris's—ones where he "just doesn't get it" and seems unnecessarily headed for trouble—that send parents into rescue mode. You find yourself, like Doris, anxious about a potential consequence that appears imminent and damaging—an unpaid debt that will destroy your transitioner's fledgling credit rating (and perhaps yours, if you have cosigned a note) or result in a car's being repossessed, a legal entanglement that could create a criminal record, a personal failure that might trigger a relapse of chemical abuse. Or for Doris, her son's unpaid speeding tickets that could result in the loss of a driver's license, likely derailing his tentative educational progress.

What is the difference between parental support and parental enabling? If you provide free room and board, are you supporting or enabling? If you subsidize transportation and phone service—support or enabling? If you once more provide a little cash to tide him over until his next paycheck—support or enabling?

It's impossible to say whether any of these instances qualify as support or enabling *until we look at what your transitioner does with the help that's offered.* The presumed parental intention in each of these examples is to be supportive, but it's the *impact* on the transitioner, not the *intention* of the parent, that answers the question of support versus enabling.

Kaylee's parents, when she maxed out her credit card as a first-year college student, bailed her out to the tune of five hundred dollars or so. Their intention was support, the thought process being that this first financial crisis of her young life would provide a valuable learning experience all by itself. After all, Kaylee seemed to own her mistake and was appropriately repentant. Personally (and professionally), I think they made the right decision. When she repeated her money mismanagement her second year, they changed their thinking and required her to pay them back for covering her overages. Again, smart parenting. They recognized that a second free bailout would amount to enabling rather than support. And when in her third year she created the financial mess that led her to my office, they again held her accountable for her spending and shut down her credit card account. Again—smart parenting, escalating consequences and refusing to support an emerging pattern of financial irresponsibility. Kaylee, the last I heard (and not surprising, given her parents' pattern of positive interventions), is now a college graduate with a good job—and a respectable credit score.

This question—to bail out or not to bail out—is one I have encountered dozens of times with parents of financially immature transitioners. One sad outcome, quite different from Kaylee's, involves two parents for whom I have served as a family psychological consultant for many years. They are about my age, and I've long felt a special fondness for both of them. They worked hard to support their four children, all of whom are now grown. Their youngest son went through a series of financial crises very similar to Kaylee's. One of the reasons I like them is that I identified with them. Like myself, they tended to be hard on themselves but found it painful to be hard on their children. They bailed this particular child out of financial crises (beginning, just like Kaylee, with a maxed-out first credit card) that escalated over time. If we were to graph the dollar amount of each successive financial crisis, the line would resemble a classic growth curve in an economics textbook. Five hundred dollars became $1,000 (a post-college summer spent unemployed), which escalated to $5,000 (to help clean up his credit score), which found its way over time to $12,000 (a failed business venture), and now, twenty years into the growth curve, has flattened out with the $40,000 down payment on his home, which he will repay in full once his latest business venture turns a profit. And this son—I have met him several times over the years—is not a sociopathic bloodsucker. He's talented, bordering on brilliant, he's appreciative, he's relational. But he's also living in a personal world shaped by unwise, unlimited parental financial support.

I've encountered a similar support/enabling parenting dilemma many times regarding whether—and to what extent—to rescue a transitioner from legal problems. This is a tough issue, as most loving parents do not want to see their kids left at the mercy of a legal system that can be capricious, random, and unnecessarily punitive. Remember the high school student I mentioned back in chapter 3? He was visiting his older brother for a "little sibs" weekend at college when he got himself into trouble for urinating in public (against the side of a building, away from campus traffic). He was in danger of being charged with an offense that could have resulted in his being labeled a sexual offender. His parents lawyered up, and I enthusiastically supported their doing so. Had it been one of my kids, I would have sold everything I owned and mortgaged the house to provide them with the finest legal support I could afford. Sometimes we rescue our kids without even a second thought.

But that's not always where I stand on legal entanglements.

Remember Gordon from chapter 7, the disorganized and irresponsible college student whose parents oscillated predictably between chewing him out and bailing him out every time he let something slide? After an unsuccessful first semester, Gordon's parents situated him on the second floor of a rental duplex just off campus. This home was in a neighborhood that was changing from family residential to college-student rental. As the neighborhood was in flux, longtime residents increasingly called the police to complain about weekend-night shenanigans. One evening in spring, two policemen sauntered down Gordon's driveway and into his backyard, where he and several friends were chatting casually between taking hits on a bong that sat on a table among their circle of lawn chairs. An appearance in court, a mandated drug evaluation, and maybe a course of outpatient substance abuse counseling would have been just what the doctor (who happened to be me) ordered. But no: His parents lawyered up, and also knew people who knew people, and Gordon was out of his jam scot-free. That's not support; that's enabling.

If you find yourself in one of these support/enabling dilemmas, here's a rule of thumb: If your transitioner is facing up to the challenges of becoming an adult—the developmental tasks outlined in Part II—then the help you provide almost certainly qualifies as *support*. They don't have to be doing a perfect job of it. None of us grew up in a straight line. Two steps forward and one step back is more than acceptable. Look at the overall longer-term pattern of your child's development. My motto is "As long as they're taking on the challenges of growing toward adulthood, as long as they're learning something valuable, something that will help them arrive at age thirty or thirty-five with a backpack filled with learning experiences and life lessons, as long as they're making progress—give them your support."

On the other hand, if your best efforts to be helpful somehow end up making it easier for your transitioner to avoid these challenges, if you find yourself looping repeatedly through the same sequence of dropped ball/neglected responsibility/parent bailout, if you find yourself crossing your fingers and praying that *this time* he or she finally *gets it*—then you're probably *enabling*.

The conundrum is this: Initially, all you have to go on are your good intentions. You can't possibly know whether you're supporting or enabling until you see the results of your efforts, and by that time—sadly—it can be difficult to reverse direction. So having unwittingly enabled your struggling transitioner, you throw up your hands and wait for the next crisis, when you face the same conundrum all over again. Before we get to the important business of escaping the enabling trap, let's take a look at how parents get stuck in the first place.

The Instinct to Protect

How do parents trap themselves into patterns of enabling their struggling transitioners? There are two common ways. The first results from a parent's natural instinct to protect children from danger. For most of us, this instinct doesn't just disappear when our children turn eighteen. Indeed, my own children are well into mature adulthood, with careers and families of their own, and don't really need my help. But from time to time I still have to check myself when I think I know something that could help them avoid unpleasant outcomes. It's a natural impulse when you love your children—to want to help them, regardless of their actual need.

Yet by the same token, a parent's protective impulse can easily lead him or her to underestimate the child's resiliency. You've probably heard the expression *helicopter parent*—the parent who intercedes with her child's high school teacher (or her college professor or even her employer) to plead for some better outcome and protect the child from disappointment and failure. Almost everyone agrees that helicopter parenting is a bad thing, so it's not surprising that parents rarely see their own parenting in this way. But helicopter parenting is mostly a matter of natural parental protectiveness gone awry.

The cultural anthropologist David Lancy, who spent his career studying parenting across cultures, believes that this "natural parental protectiveness" is not so natural after all, but a product of several unique aspects of developed, Westernized society. Lancy observed that parenting in indigenous cultures is characterized by an attitude he labels *benign neglect*, where children are valued more according to their utility and potential contribution to family and community. This stands in sharp contrast to Western cultures, in which children are granted a privileged status, intrinsically meriting the highest levels of protection and investment. Lancy speculates that this elevated status may reflect the fact that, at least in contemporary middle- and upper-middle-class society, children are *intended* additions to the family, *chosen and planned* instead of arriving, welcomed or not, according to some divine or natural plan. This heightening of intentionality and emotional investment has, according to Lancy, fostered a dramatic increase in parental anxiety and spawned a contemporary epidemic of perfectionistic parenting. This is a harsh judgment, perhaps, but one deserving our consideration and reflection.

Lancy's insight has been echoed and amplified by the teacher and journalist Jessica Lahey, whose wonderful book, *The Gift of Failure*, describes it in excruciating detail:

> Out of love and desire to protect our children's self-esteem, we have bulldozed every uncomfortable bump and obstacle out of their way, clearing the manicured path we hoped would lead to success and happiness. Unfortunately, in doing so we have deprived our children of the most important lessons of childhood. The setbacks, mistakes, miscalculations, and failures we have shoved out of our children's way are the very experiences that teach them how to be resourceful, persistent, innovative, and resilient citizens of this world.

We need to listen carefully to both Lancy and Lahey. The first step in escaping the enabling trap is to look squarely in the mirror and ask yourself: "Am I underestimating my transitioner's resiliency? In protecting him or her from an 'unacceptable consequence,' am I really protecting *myself* from the pain of watching him or her struggle, and depriving him or her of an opportunity to learn an important lesson about how the world works—and what they can do to help themselves?"

Catastrophizing

The second way that parents slide into enabling—an outgrowth of the first—has to do with what cognitive behavioral therapists call *catastrophizing*, a tendency to look at challenging situations in terms of the worst possible outcomes. Doris feared that letting her son face the consequences of his unpaid speeding tickets might ruin his life. Well . . . that's one possibility, but hardly the most likely. But this was Doris's catastrophic vision, and against my advice, she went and paid the fines on his behalf.

When I meet parents caught in the enabling trap, it's inevitably the case that they are paralyzed by a vision of their transitioner's developmental collapse. They see themselves as the bulwark standing between their child and disaster—a missed registration deadline, an accumulation of overdraft fees, a bad credit rating, a court appearance for marijuana possession, and so on. Cognitive behavioral therapy is built upon a simple but very powerful insight—namely, that our thoughts are a form of *behavior*. Our thinking isn't just a window on the truth, which is what most us of tend to assume as we go about our daily lives. Thinking, like all behavior, is subject to assumptions and habits of distortion. Long-standing dispositions such as optimism and pessimism are familiar examples of the way that thinking can develop a bias consistent with an individual's personality.

Because of the protective slant of most parents' dispositions toward their children, there is a built-in bias to worry about all the things that could go wrong—and this is especially true if you are the sort of person vulnerable to feeling anxiety. I'm such a person, and when my daughter (whom you've met previously in these pages) was in her early thirties, she finally took me aside, put her finger in my chest, and stated forcefully: "Dad! PLEASE stop reminding me to put on my seat belt every time I get into a car. I know enough to use a seat belt!" Of course I instantly realized the absurdity of this out-of-date parenting tic and stopped my annoying behavior immediately.

Catastrophizing works by taking this protective instinct and embellishing it into a full-blown disaster fantasy, which quickly takes on the pall of likelihood or inevitability. Addressing your transitioner's challenging situation can begin to feel like getting onto an airplane with a Technicolor newsreel of every plane crash scene you've ever heard of looping through your brain. The more you think about it, the more it begins to feel like a high probability that this flight is destined to crash.

That's catastrophizing!

The counter-dote (there really isn't an antidote, if you're inclined toward anxiety) of catastrophizing is, after a series of slow, deep breaths, to walk through (or talk through with someone more objective than yourself) the situation and identify the *range* of possible outcomes, with an eye to realistically assessing their relative likelihoods. If Doris had walked through this exercise (or if I had been sharp enough that particular morning to walk her through it!), she might have realized that students with suspended licenses are usually given limited driving privileges that include driving back and forth to school, particularly in local suburban courts where magistrates typically feel some measure of responsibility toward taxpaying citizens. This sort of reconsideration would likely have helped Doris to let Jeremy face the consequences of his refusal to deal with his speeding tickets. No doubt he'd have been impacted by the heavy fines and penalties, but that would have been a good thing. It's very unlikely that he would have had to quit school, and I'm certain he wouldn't have ended up living under a bridge.

It takes courage to parent a struggling transitioner. It also involves taking risks, allowing the chips to fall where they may, and doing one's best to help convert the "catastrophe" into a life lesson.

With enabling, parents do just the opposite. Despite their best intentions, they get themselves caught in a pattern of "helpfulness" that not only doesn't help but actually becomes counterproductive. The psychology behind this phenomenon is interesting, so let's look closer at how parental helpfulness can unintentionally fuel transitioner irresponsibility.

When Being Helpful Isn't Helpful

Gordon in chapter 7 had parents, Jack and Myrna, who worked assiduously—and unsuccessfully—to shape him into an adult. Gordon managed this task himself only after his parents reallocated their energies toward their grandchildren, and withdrew their unhelpful "help."

As extreme as Gordon's pattern of irresponsibility had been, the dynamic of his relationship with his parents is common in the families of struggling transitioners. The more his parents tried to help him out, the more he took their help for granted. And the more he took their help for granted, the more he neglected the management of his own affairs. This is what happened with Doris and her son, too. Paying his speeding tickets was just one incident in a long line of compensations she made for his neglect of responsibilities. He could afford his obliviousness *only* because he had a mother who was so "helpful."

If you've got a transitioner in your life who is even a little like Jeremy or Gordon, it's a good bet that you're caught in the enabling trap. In his attempts to avoid the responsibilities of growing up, your transitioner has taken advantage of your good intentions, your loving protection, and your sincere efforts to help. Your efforts to induce, motivate, inspire, or mandate responsible behavior may actually serve as an integral part of your transitioner's continuing immaturity and avoidance of responsibility.

Like it or not, you may have become part of the problem.

The enabling trap is one more expression of the tangled boundaries of the outmoded parent-adolescent relational paradigm. The trap is sealed by the tacit underlying ground rules that properly organize and constrain the relationships of parents and their adolescent children, but are unhelpfully carried forward into the emerging adulthood years.

Here's a thought experiment that illustrates the point. Imagine that you've got the seventeen-year-old from hell living in your home. They neglect schoolwork, use drugs, ignore house rules, are rude and uncivil, and take everything you provide for granted. The bad news (or the good news, depending on how you look at it) is that you are still obligated to parent that seventeen-year-old. Maybe you'll go to the extreme of placing him or her in some sort of treatment program, or involving the police if there are threats of violence. But you're still required to carry on, however unsuccessfully, trying your best to help that teenager to survive adolescence. Your material support is not open to negotiation. Maybe you take away the cell phone, withhold the car keys, or turn off the Wi-Fi, but you can't even think about asking them to pay rent or to help pay for groceries or to find another place to live. Plain and simple, the relational paradigm of adolescence *requires* you to provide for your child as best you can.

Most families perpetuate this relational paradigm well past its expiration date at age eighteen. The normal progression is that the paradigm changes over a four- to six-year period, with the child morphing gradually from an adolescent into an emerging adult, while the parent morphs in parallel fashion from a supervisor-caretaker to a consultant. But with struggling transitioners, that natural evolution breaks down, and both transitioner and parent are trapped in the time warp of adolescence.

When I meet parents caught in the enabling trap, I frequently find that they are polarized around opposing temperaments and philosophies. Ricky's parents (whom we met earlier in this chapter) were a textbook example. His father wanted to throw him out of the house and change the locks. His mother confessed to being the softy, confiding privately that she slipped Ricky the occasional twenty bucks when he was short. Each parent resented and held the other responsible for the perpetuation of their son's adolescence.

The fascinating thing about this sort of polarization is that each parent holds a portion of the solution. If parents are going to shift gears and move toward a new relational paradigm—one that will foster, not impede, their struggling transitioner's development— they need to blend the wisdom of their polarized positions. Ricky's father realizes that they can't continue providing material support carte blanche; there has to be a limit. He understands that material support for a transitioner should *not* be unconditional, the way it is for an adolescent (emotional support, yes; material support, no). His mother understands that behind Ricky's headstrong defensiveness lives a scared kid, one who feels overmatched by the demands of the adult world—and who needs to feel love and support from mom and dad.

The challenge for Ricky's parents—and for most of the parents I have introduced in these pages—is to blend the clarity of reasonable terms and limits for material support with the warmth and commitment of enduring love. This is challenging but possible. The relational paradigm of emerging adulthood is significantly different from the parent-adolescent paradigm of the enabling trap. Specifically, there are three defining features that differentiate the emerging adult paradigm of financial/material support from the paradigms of childhood and adolescence.

A New Paradigm for Material Support

The first difference is that essential material support—food, clothing, shelter, education, and so forth—is (or should become) discretionary in emerging adulthood, whereas it is obligatory in adolescence. I made the point back in chapter 2 that one of the underlying changes that occurs in the parent-child relationship after high school is that it becomes *voluntary on both sides*, even though it can take a while for this subtle but important shift to be felt as real and acknowledged by all concerned. Applied to the domain of material support, this shift means that it is a legitimate matter of *choice*, on both sides of the relationship, as to whether parents continue to provide for these needs, and whether kids accept what's provided. When transitioners are going about the business of growing up and preparing for the future, this typically isn't much of an issue, except as it relates to parents' available financial resources. (In many families, there are open, non-conflictual discussions about what parents can and cannot afford in terms of help with college tuition, or that rent is expected once a graduate is working full time.) These are unselfconscious conversations about financial realities, rather than calculated strategies designed to break outdated patterns of adolescent financial dependency.

But in other families, where transitioners are not addressing the curriculum of growing up and adolescent patterns of financial dependence have outlived their use-by date, the idea that financial support is discretionary requires artful attention. For starters, parents need to change their own outdated habits of thinking about ongoing, no-strings-attached financial support, and this frequently proves more challenging than parents expect. I have many times fielded the utterly sincere question "Am I a *horrible parent* if I stop paying for his cell phone/gas/Netflix subscription, or if I (gasp!) ask for monthly rent?" The answer, of course, is *no!* But many parents find this obvious answer harder to process emotionally than intellectually. The solution to this conundrum has already been presented in the previous three chapters. Don't think of these financial changes as essentially *financial*. They're not. The reason you want her to begin paying her own cell phone bill or to contribute to the monthly grocery fund isn't because you need the money (unless, of course, it *is* because you need the money, which, as I pointed out earlier, is a much easier conversation to have); the reason is because you want your *relationship* to feel more grown-up and mutual. You want it to be better for both of you.

When parents decide to continue providing material support, the proper test for exercising this discretion is whether doing so facilitates or impedes growth and development. If your twenty-something asked for a thousand dollars for a trip to a casino, you'd likely say no. On the other hand, if he or she asked for a thousand dollars to pay for a prep course for the Law School Admission Test or for a community college course in auto mechanics, assuming you have the funds available, you'd likely help out. If your transitioner understands that material support is discretionary ("*Thank you*, Mom and Dad, for putting me up while I look for a job! *Thank you*, Mom and Dad, for lending me the money to get my landscaping business up and running."), then your relationship is probably on solid ground. But as we saw with Jeremy (unpaid speeding tickets) and Jake (missing car payments) and Nick (treatment of parents' home and possessions as if they were his own), struggling transitioners frequently don't regard material support as discretionary—they take it for granted. And the main reason they don't see that support as discretionary is because their parents *themselves* don't regard it as discretionary.

The second definitive characteristic of material support in the emerging adult paradigm—and a close corollary of the first—is that it's transactional. Transactional means that financial and material support is framed as a two-way street. When material support is provided, it should be provided with contingencies—if-then arrangements that establish expectations and responsibilities on both sides of a relationship. "I'll pay for your education, *provided that* you do the work of being a student." "We'll provide you with room and board at home, *provided that* you follow house rules and do your share around the house." "I'll help you buy a car, *provided that* you use it to find employment and get yourself back and forth to work."

Setting up contingencies is a natural part of parenting, regardless of the child's age. For a young child, we make dessert contingent upon eating her vegetables. For a teenager, we make weekend privileges or use of the car contingent upon household civility or maintaining acceptable grades. Contingencies with transitioners have an entirely different character than they do with younger children. For one thing, there are much bigger things being held contingent—not dessert or weekend privileges, but ongoing material support: tuition, housing, financial aid. Here's the key difference: With transitioners, contingencies need to reflect the *mutuality* of the relationship, resembling more an arrangement between adults than the obligatory caretaking of younger children or teenagers.

Many parents of struggling transitioners tell me, "We've set up contingencies, but they don't work! We tell him/her what's expected, but she/he hasn't come through." This complaint is a sure sign that while you may be *verbally* invoking the emerging adult paradigm, you and your transitioner are *behaviorally* operating under the perseverated paradigm of adolescence.

Transitioners trapped in the adolescent paradigm typically regard their parents—to invoke a slightly exaggerated image—as ATMs. With ATMs, you enter a secret code and out pops money. It's like magic. And the "secret codes" that adolescent-stage transitioners routinely employ (secret even to themselves) include a wide range of behaviors, some of which are constructive (for example, getting good grades) and some of which are not (for example, passivity, inducing guilt, demanding, or bullying). Most don't like to think about it and don't. They simply take the availability of material support for granted.

To move beyond the ATM model, we want transitioners to regard their parents' material support—again invoking an analogy—more the way a small business owner regards his or her banker. That is, we want them to regard material support as part of a two-way relationship—one in which they, too, have obligations. To facilitate this fundamental change in transitioner thinking, you must also learn to change your thinking about material support. This shift involves making material support contingent upon the transitioner's holding up his or her end of the relationship. Most parents already know this intuitively, but don't apply the principle with enough commitment or consistency. There's nothing cold or uncaring about making material support contingent; it's simply a way of insisting that the relationship be organized in a fashion that supports emerging adult behavior.

The third defining characteristic of material support in the emerging adult paradigm is that it takes into account the legitimate and healthy self-interests of parents. This is crucial. In any mature and healthy relationship between adults (including emerging adults), there exists, as I have stressed repeatedly, the quality of *mutuality*, which was discussed in chapter 5. Mutuality means that each party in the relationship regards and respects the other's legitimate self-interests. And you can't expect your transitioner to respect your self-interests if you're not clear about them yourself.

Let's take the example of house rules to illustrate this point. Suppose your transitioner is living under your roof and you have established the following house rules: no staying up all night and sleeping into the afternoon; no bringing your boyfriend/girlfriend to spend the night; no pot smoking. If you've set these rules because you are trying to regulate your transitioner's behavior, then you are pursuing a supervisory parenting agenda, which means that you're operating under the outmoded paradigm of parenting an adolescent. In adolescence, most of us would agree that a parent's job description includes attempting to curtail presumably unhealthy behaviors. With your transitioner, as opposed to your adolescent, this sort of parenting agenda is one more instance of tangled boundaries. After all, your transitioner's sleep needs, sex life, and substance use are really *his or her* business, not yours.

So what *is* your business?

In the emerging adulthood paradigm, the adolescent parenting agenda is (or should be) replaced by an agenda that takes into account the parents' legitimate self-interests. After all, you are entitled to be comfortable in your own home, and you don't need to explain or justify any house rules established to assure your own comfort. If the same house rules were established—no staying out all night without giving notice; no bringing your boyfriend/girlfriend to spend the night; no pot smoking—*not* to regulate your transitioner's behavior or to teach them what you believe are desirable values, but to make *you* comfortable under your own roof, you are operating under a more age-appropriate paradigm. This may sound like I'm splitting hairs, but I assure you that is not the case. The same house rules, established under different relational paradigms, yield different results. Your transitioner will quickly sense the difference between an agenda designed to regulate his or her behavior and an agenda that is designed to ensure your legitimate needs for comfort.

Here's a case in point. I recently consulted with parents and their twenty-four-year-old son, who was living at home. They had been locked in an ongoing battle about his pot smoking (often at home) for several years. When his parents shifted from "No pot smoking! It's unhealthy, it makes you lazy, and it's illegal" (an adolescent parenting agenda that I wholeheartedly endorse—for adolescents) to "We disapprove of your pot smoking, but realize you're going to do what you're going to do. We think it's a bad decision, but we concede that it's *your* decision. But NO POT SMOKING IN OUR HOME" (a legitimate self-interest/house rules agenda), his behavior changed dramatically. The parents' agenda (and their son most definitely picked up on this) switched from one of trying to parent him to one of insisting upon their right to be comfortable in their own home. The first agenda triggered his long-standing adolescent tendency to engage in a power struggle whenever he sensed that someone was trying to control him. The second—the house rules agenda—he didn't like but conceded was legitimate. He did indeed stop smoking pot at home, and their distinct impression, when last we spoke, was that he had curtailed his use generally. This seemingly subtle distinction is *not* subtle to a transitioner. It represents the difference between being treated like an adolescent and being treated like an adult. This young man felt the paradigm shift, and his behavior shifted accordingly.

Financial and material support can serve as a deadweight anchor in an outmoded adolescent parenting paradigm. But by the same token, it is often the central arena for resetting the ground rules of the parent-transitioner relationship and triggering attitudes and behavior more fitting to emergent adulthood.

Parents should know:

- Talk with your transitioner—in real, concrete terms—about money and its role in your (and their) life.
- Before you jump in to "save" your transitioner, consider whether your assistance is supporting (productive) or enabling (unhelpful) him or her. It all has to do with what your child does with the help that's offered.

Chapter 11

Communication and Emotional Support

Staying Connected Even
When Times Are Tough

I f you've got a transitioner in your family who is well on his or her way toward adulthood, then the business of communicating and providing emotional support is a relatively straightforward matter. You offer advice, encouragement, wisdom, and the occasional kick in the proverbial rear end, and your transitioner (perhaps with undertones of appreciation and occasionally resentment) starts looking for that job, buckles down in school, or begins to help clean up the kitchen after dinner.

The situation with struggling transitioners, however, is precisely the opposite. She doesn't ask for advice, even though you may know exactly what she needs to do. And when you offer uninvited input, she becomes combative or withdrawn, or blames you for whatever problem is at hand. You feel frustrated and powerless and wind up walking on eggshells in your own home. Do you bug her about the parking tickets or the car payment or the unenthusiastic job search, even though you know that this will most likely lead to friction and further aggravation? Or do you bite your tongue, cross your fingers, and hope that somehow she will get her act together?

How Communication Breaks Down

I recently met with parents who were struggling with this dilemma. I'd been seeing their nineteen-year-old son in therapy for several months, and on this day I had brought them together in my office. Alex presented a profile that matches almost perfectly the composite described in Part I. He had made a mess of his first year in college, barely avoiding academic probation, and throughout the summer had steadfastly refused to sit down with his parents for an adult-to-adult discussion about his first-year difficulties or his plans for a more successful second year.

By his mom and dad's account, they had tried repeatedly to have this conversation, employing every approach they could conjure. They'd been matter-of-fact; they'd been insistent; they'd been gentle and supportive; they'd even been businesslike, insisting at one point that he submit a "business plan" for his upcoming academic year. None of these efforts had led to the sort of adult-level discussion that (1) they're entitled to, given that they're footing the bill, and (2) they knew would be useful to Alex by crystallizing his assessment of his poor performance and formulating a viable plan for the upcoming year.

Instead of a frank sit-down, what they had gotten—and I observed this in my office, too—was deflection, avoidance, minimization, and irritated bristling: "I've *told* you, I'm on top of it! Why do you keep hassling me and rubbing my nose in it?" At this point he turned to me and exclaimed, "See what I mean? *This* is what I have to put up with!" The family's communication had broken down, and the parents' best efforts to provide support were having the opposite effect on Alex.

Alex's history sheds light on the communication breakdowns between many struggling transitioners and their parents. Alex was one of those bright underachieving kids who struggled "mysteriously" in school through the primary grades. He was slow to learn to read and had difficulty with higher-level reading even after he had mastered the rudiments. He was terribly disorganized and therefore easily overwhelmed by school assignments. Not surprising, he came to find school intolerably boring and over time lost interest in all things academic. In sixth grade, however, he was diagnosed with a mild form of dyslexia and with attention deficit hyperactivity disorder (ADHD).

This is not an unusual history in today's day and age. I've known hundreds of kids with similar developmental and academic histories. After Alex was diagnosed at age twelve, his story took a positive turn. His parents procured supplemental services for his reading, got appropriate and effective medication for his ADHD, and had him placed on an Individualized Education Plan (IEP). More so than many kids with this constellation of learning challenges and commensurate supports, Alex responded fabulously. His performance in school improved dramatically, as did his overall attitude toward academics. In his own words: "I began to feel a lot better about myself."

Alex continued on his IEP through ninth grade, and was ratcheted back to 504 accommodations (which he rarely utilized) for the remainder of his high school career. With occasional hiccups, Alex did well enough to finish high school and get admitted to a good college. But what often happens to people like Alex—those with a history that includes academic frustration and failure and an unarticulated visceral experience of inadequacy and shame—is that they are vulnerable to an "echo chamber" effect whenever they encounter new challenges to their academic competency. This is a similar but less intense version of the flashback phenomenon that occurs to people with posttraumatic stress disorder (PTSD). When some new circumstances simulate the earlier overwhelming situation, emotions from the earlier situation come flooding back.

For Alex, this happened in his first year in college. In several challenging classes he found himself emotionally back in grade school: feeling confused, overwhelmed, and incompetent. And just as in grade school, he didn't have words for much of this, only intense feelings that triggered his old coping mechanism of withdrawing energy and interest from the challenges at hand. The concrete result was several incompletes for courses he gave up on. In his individual sessions with me, all of this came pouring out, as Alex began to find the words for how "stupid" and inadequate he felt, and how much he "hated" himself for being "so incompetent."

In light of this history, Alex's strange refusal to entertain his parents' reasonable requests for a straightforward discussion of his performance and plans began to make sense. With me, essentially a stranger, Alex could summon the courage to look within and find the words for what he was feeling. But with his parents, he couldn't get past feeling that he was a failure, a screw-up, and that he had disappointed them. And until he spent time with me, he couldn't even find words for why their inquiries made him so angry.

As a family, Alex and his parents, in spite of their collective good intentions, had suffered a serious communication breakdown. The more they inquired, the more irritable and withdrawn he became. The more uncommunicative he became, the more anxious his parents became about his welfare and his future. His mother's anxiety expressed itself in her intensified efforts to "get her foot in the door," communication-wise. "Leave me alone!" he would explode at her, "Stop asking me all those questions!"

His father had a more realistic concern about course selections Alex had made for the upcoming year, and whether Alex had thought through these choices realistically. His concern was that Alex was taking on (as he had in his first year) courses that played to his academic weaknesses, rather than to his strengths. This was a conversation that Alex needed to have with someone, but whenever his father raised the issue, Alex was flooded with a vague sense of his own insufficiency. At a not-quite-verbalized level, Alex knew he was a poor planner, but felt so ashamed about it that he recoiled from any conversation that made his feelings of incompetence (I prefer "pre-competence") more acute.

This was not a case of parents doing anything "wrong." In fact, everything they were trying to do—from my vantage point, if not from Alex's—was reasonable, well intended, and potentially helpful. The thing that was missing—and this is the norm, not the exception—was a full appreciation of Alex's inner-world experience. They proceeded, like most well-intentioned parents, on a basis of rational, real-world problem-solving. Alex, on the other hand, was proceeding on the basis of his echo chamber of damaged self-esteem and his underlying feelings of inadequacy. The task at hand, at least as I defined it for them, was much trickier than the simple conversation they sought. It was more a matter of bridging two different realities—Alex's inner world and their outer world—and creating a new space where each could begin to grasp and appreciate the other.

This is what I engineered for Alex and his parents in my office by acting as a translator. With all four of us in the room, I said to Alex: "Alex, tell *me* what you want your parents to hear."

He complied: "To leave me alone. I want them to stop pushing this like I don't know what I'm doing. They treat me like an incompetent."

"May I translate freely?" I asked him, to which he nodded. I turned to his mom and dad and said something like this: "What Alex wants you to know is how awful he feels about screwing up last year. He hates the feeling of having disappointed you, and he wants more than anything to show you, this upcoming year, that he can pull it off on his own. I think he's saying that if he has the conversation you've been asking for, it's going to feel like you fixed the problem, rather than like *he* fixed the problem."

I then turned to Alex and asked, "Am I close?" He nodded slowly, head down.

I then did the same exercise with his parents: "Tell me what you want Alex to hear." They essentially repeated what they had been saying throughout the session.

His mother: "I just want to know what's going on in your life."

His father: "I just need to know that you're thinking through your plans for this next year. This could be the do-or-die year for your future."

Me to Alex, again translating: "Your mom wants you to know how scary it is for her when she doesn't know you're okay. And how could she know otherwise? You don't talk to her! She wants you to know that when you ask her to leave you alone, it just makes her feel confused and scared. You're asking her to do the impossible. And your dad is trying to tell you how much he wants you to pull it off—to solve it yourself, just the way you want. But he's a dad, so it's really difficult for him to just stand back and not share with you what he knows about how the world works. Your dad probably learned things the hard way, and he wants you not to have it so hard yourself." Like Alex, his parents nodded that what I said felt true, even if they hadn't put it quite the way I did.

Then I gave Alex one of my favorite set pieces: the "crazy parent" speech.

"Look, Alex, *all* parents are crazy. Your parents are crazy; my parents were crazy; I was crazy when I was raising my kids; and you're going to be crazy when you have kids. It's just what happens when you love someone as desperately as parents love their kids. So even when we get it wrong, you've got to cut us some slack. Your parents would stand on their heads and spit jelly beans if they thought that would help. You don't have to like it, but can you see that this is where they're coming from?"

"I never thought of it that way before," he replied softly.

"Why don't you tell them what your plan is for next year," I prodded, because I knew that he *had* thought a lot about it and did indeed have a well-thought-out plan for how he was going to approach the upcoming year differently.

He did; they listened; and I could see the tension leave their faces and shoulders as he spoke.

Communication and Emotional Support

Twenty-year-old George was another therapy client of mine, and his psychological profile was similar to many of the young people I've introduced in these pages. George fought through a significant depression in his last two years of high school, coinciding with his mother's tragic and untimely death due to uterine cancer. That was ancient history by the time I met him, but George was still struggling with getting himself unstuck and preparing for a future. He was two years out from high school graduation and hadn't done much of anything productive since. In therapy, George had begun to come to terms with his anxieties and his lack of confidence and had been accepted at a four-year university. In the summer before George went to college, the topic of our sessions was his experience of his father's efforts to be "helpful," which George—no surprise—experienced as not helpful at all. George complained that his father had no faith in him, would not acknowledge the progress he'd made, and was critical of his every move. In short, George experienced his father's involvement as decidedly unsupportive, and this threatened to erode George's emergent motivation and his tentative self-confidence.

However, there was a problem with this picture—George's portrayal of his father was objectively inaccurate. I had recently invited George's father to my office, and he told a very different story: George needed to get a summer job in order to have spending money while in college, but the job search was in slow motion. George also had a ream of paperwork to complete for the college—course selection, health insurance, dorm and food plan selection, and so on. The deadline for their submission was approaching, but George hadn't yet attended to them. George knew he had to master these minor adult-world challenges— finding a job, filling out paperwork, meeting a deadline—but was intimidated by the "grown-up" nature of these responsibilities. Why? Because like most twenty-year-olds, George was inexperienced and naive about how the adult world works, and this fact left him feeling inadequate and embarrassed. Rather than face it, he perpetuated the paradigm of adolescence: He both counted on and resented his father's intervention.

The Anatomy of Emotional Support

Was George's dad's behavior *un*supportive? If we take an "objective" point of view, I think we'd all say no. He was only trying to help. But if we're going to unlock the secrets of providing emotional support to *struggling* transitioners, we've got to throw objectivity out the window. In this instance, effective emotional support isn't determined strictly by dad's good intentions. A parent's involvement isn't effectively supportive *unless the transitioner experiences it as such.* To crack that code, we've got to look at support from the inside out—from the vantage point of the transitioner's subjective experience.

Gloria, nineteen, is a perfect example. Very bright and with excellent SAT scores, Gloria entered a top-flight university after high school. But Gloria suffered from a significant anxiety disorder and found the competitive atmosphere of college overwhelming. Following a harrowing first year, she lobbied her parents for a belated gap year, which felt more within her comfort zone. Her parents initially resisted this, but when Gloria became intransigent and flatly refused to return for her sophomore year, they relented.

Gloria had done an eleventh-grade semester at a farm school that partnered with her high school, and had loved the experience. She wanted to do something similar now, and her research turned up a substantial yearlong internship opportunity at an integrated botanical garden–arboretum conservatory not too far from her home. The real conflict arose as her internship drew to a close, when her parents expected she would return to her four-year university program. Gloria pleaded for their understanding, and lobbied for their support for attending an associate's-level horticultural program at our local community college. Her parents felt strongly that she was selling herself short, interpreting, perhaps correctly, that Gloria was making a choice based upon her anxieties rather than heartfelt career aspirations. They brought her to me hoping that I could help her get on top of her anxiety and return to her university studies.

Their desires were reasonable, by my estimation. Gloria, I thought, would make a wonderful horticulturalist, albeit atypical, given that she had read most of Shakespeare and translated bits of Goethe from the original German. Her parents brought these facts to my attention, hoping to recruit me to their (again, very reasonable) agenda that she return to university.

After spending a month getting to know Gloria and her parents, I counseled just the opposite. Gloria's anxiety was more than just a symptom. It was, temporarily at least, a part of her identity—part of the way that she distinguished safety from danger—and I felt it important that her parents meet her in *her* world, rather than demanding that she join them in theirs. Anxiety for most of us is about getting out of our comfort zone. It's a signal that's triggered when entering new and unfamiliar territory, telling me that I cannot take my security and competence for granted. People learn to manage anxiety by pushing beyond their familiar comfort zones—a method psychologists call *exposure*—expanding that zone to include new territory. But it's important that this exposure occur in manageable doses and not too far away from reliable sources of support. The right balance of exposure and support allows the new challenge to be mastered, gradually expanding an individual's range of comfort and confidence.

University was just too big a step beyond Gloria's comfort zone, regardless of her capabilities.

Gloria's parents accepted my advice and enrolled her in a horticultural program for the following year. Gloria's anxiety lessened almost immediately, by virtue of feeling met and supported by her parents. Her attitude toward school improved dramatically, too, and she performed well. At the conclusion of her program, she took a job in a high-end garden center and worked for a full year.

The heroes in this story, to my mind, were Gloria's parents. They found themselves in the position that every parent of every talented struggling transitioner has had to face. They "knew better"; they knew what their daughter was capable of and yet they were confronted with their daughter telling them she wasn't ready to go there. I know these parents well and hold them in my heart as iconic: They put their (very justified and reasonable) hopes and expectations aside and met their daughter at her own growing developmental edge, supporting her to take the step she was ready to take.

I received an email from them around the time Gloria turned twenty-two. She had come to them and declared her readiness to return to a university degree program, and was confident and thriving at the time of their message. Three years later, to the month, I heard from them again—this time in the form of an invitation to her university graduation. I'm not sure where she's heading as I write this, but if I ever need a Shakespeare scholar to plan my garden, or a garden specialist to enthrall me for hours on end with reflections on the adolescent developmental implications of *Romeo and Juliet*, I have an idea whom to call.

The subjective experience of emotional support involves two essential components: feeling *understood* and feeling *accepted*. Feeling understood is just what it says: having the experience that other people *get me*, that they grasp and appreciate what I'm going through *from my point of view*. This doesn't mean that their point of view is identical to mine, just that they understand where I'm coming from. When someone says to me, "I see how you would feel that way," I feel understood. Perhaps not perfectly, but enough that I feel supported.

Feeling *accepted* is closely related to feeling understood. It essentially means that I don't feel judged. Acceptance in this context is not the same as approval, as when someone thinks I am doing a terrific job. It's more along the lines of being found acceptable in the eyes of the other, even in the midst of whatever struggles and difficulties I may be having. Acceptance is the antidote for shame, and George was feeling shame in spades in response to his father's (and his own) disapproval and disappointment. George already knew he wasn't doing a good job; he was, after all, a *struggling* transitioner. What he needed was to feel his father's acceptance and understanding *in spite of that fact*. For George, the antidote for his shame was his father's empathy. What his father needed to do was put himself in George's shoes, to remember times in his own life when he felt overmatched and intimidated by some unfamiliar challenge. And he needed to communicate that; he needed to let George know that he could accept the fact of George's fear and intimidation. That's the essence of acceptance.

Here's what happened. I brought George and his dad together in my office to address the problem of getting George ready for school. George's dad began the session by repeating his concerns about George's future and his exasperation at George's foot-dragging. After George's dad had finished his opening statement, I asked George what he had to say and watched him sink back into his chair and hang his head, shame oozing from his pores. I then turned the conversation to George's dad, catching him off guard. "Have you ever felt overmatched?" I asked. "You know, in a new job, or something similar?"

"I thought we were here to help George," he countered.

"We are," I replied, "but I want you to trust me on this."

"Well," he began haltingly, "sure . . . yeah, I guess so."

"So tell me about it," I requested.

Dad then told me the story of his first job after college, when he had felt overwhelmed by expectations and duties that he was not prepared for. I shared with him similar experiences that I had had as a new psychologist, when people turned to me for guidance about matters I knew little about. I told him how embarrassed I was about my ignorance, how I felt like I was faking it, and how terrified I was that I might be exposed as a phony. He laughed and nodded, confiding that he had felt very much the same way. During our conversation, George didn't say a word, but he listened intently. When our conversation trailed off,

I turned to George and asked if he had known this about his dad. He smiled for the first time and shook his head slowly, saying, "No, I never knew about that."

I turned to George's dad at that point and said, "I think George feels pretty much the same way that you and I did when we were both starting out. Am I right, George?"

"Yeah," George nodded. "Pretty much."

That conversation was a turning point for George and his dad. Dad got it, and George felt relieved and understood. "Your dad can help you," I said to George. "You okay with that?"

"Yeah," he said, "I'm okay with that."

Rules to Communicate By

There are two important rules to keep in mind when you're trying to break through to a struggling transitioner.

Communication rule 1. Start with empathy. Put yourself in your child's shoes. However badly he or she may be messing up or neglecting his or her responsibilities, try to imagine what it must feel like, deep down, to be him or her. Try to remember your own insecurities and screw-ups from your younger days; try to recall what it felt like to feel challenged or overmatched by the demands of behaving like a grown-up. Once George saw that his father understood how he felt, he became much more open to his father's involvement.

Remember, too, that the essence of empathy isn't just saying the words "I understand." The essence of empathy is something you do inside; it's work you do on yourself to imagine and grasp the challenging situation and underlying feelings that may be holding your transitioner back. Even when you are forced to challenge or confront your transitioner about some serious misstep, start the communication process by mentally and emotionally gauging what he or she must be feeling inside. Start by putting yourself in their place; isn't this what you would want if you were a struggling transitioner?

Overall, I find this business of empathy to be more of a challenge for men than for women. If I had a nickel for every time I've had a man in my office—whether in family counseling, couples therapy, or individual consultation—say to me, "He/she/they want me to be more in touch with my feelings, but I just don't know what they want"—I'd have at least . . . well, maybe just enough for a nice meal or two (a nickel doesn't go as far these days!). But because men in our culture, generally speaking, are less attuned to their own emotional lives and histories (the story behind that fact is a whole other book!), they often plead no contest when accused of lacking empathy.

I've learned to offer a short-course tutorial for men who plead guilty to empathy deficiency, because I think such a deficiency is mostly an imaginary, culturally myth-driven pseudo-truism. Here's the tutorial, in the form of some of the things I say to fathers (and occasionally mothers) of struggling transitioners in need of understanding and acceptance. "Empathy does not mean that you have to feel what your kid is feeling; in fact, you don't need to be a big 'feeler' to understand other people's emotional states. Empathy is as much a matter of *intelligence and imagination* as it is of emotion. Can you *imagine* what it might feel like to be in your kid's situation? Were you ever in anything resembling your kid's situation?" (Most parents have, but have conveniently hit the memory-delete button.)

If the parent in front of me is a businessperson or a professional, I ask "How do you figure out what your customers want? What your boss wants? What your clients or patients need from you?" Most can answer those questions readily, and when they do, I push forward. "Well, if you can figure out your potential customer/boss/client/patient's experiential point of view, you can certainly apply that skill to your screwing up/dropping the ball/deeply embarrassed/somewhat defensive twenty-two-year-old." The typical response to my therapeutic diatribe is one of my favorite experiences of being a therapist. After a moment of silence, my client's eyes slowly widen and his or her head cocks slightly clockwise. There's a pause and then they say something like, "Oh . . . I hadn't looked at it that way before."

Communication rule 2. Honor boundaries. Just as we saw with issues of responsibility, motivation, and material support, clear boundaries—recognizing whose business is what—are a key to productive communication. Most of us are acutely attuned to the boundaries we have negotiated and established in various relationships. If your financial adviser asked you about your income and savings, you may or may not be comfortable with the question, but you wouldn't consider it a boundary violation. If your neighbor asked you the same question . . . well, that's another matter. And the more sensitive you consider the subject matter, the more troubled you might feel about the boundary transgression.

Transitioners are typically *much* more attuned to their relational boundaries with parents than their parents are to their own relational boundaries with transitioners. In any relationship, the party with less status and power is generally more attuned to transgressions. As a consequence, transitioners frequently experience innocent inquiries, unsolicited advice, gentle reminders, and casual observations as boundary transgressions. If your transitioner bristles when you attempt to communicate or seems overly sensitive to your observations and opinions, it's a good bet he or she experiences your communication as transgressing personal boundaries.

In your former role as supervisor-caretaker of a child or adolescent, unsolicited advice and strategic nagging were necessary and appropriate components of your job description. But if you're committed to upgrading your relationship paradigm to consultant with your emerging adult, then unsolicited advice and nagging are potential boundary violations.

Regardless of how much you think your transitioner *needs* your advice, offering it unsolicited just invites him or her to continue thinking and behaving like an adolescent. The premise of any consulting relationship is that your "client" has *requested* your input. George's dad needed to replace "Have you filled out those forms yet?" with "I know you've got a lot on your plate, and the deadline for turning in those forms is coming up quickly. Let me know if there's any way I can be helpful." That's shifting from parent as supervisor to parent as consultant. Communication in the consultant paradigm is always mindful of whose business is what, and filling out those forms or asking for his father's help was definitely George's business.

Nagging can also have the effect of prolonging the confused boundaries of adolescence. By nagging Alex to present a plan for the upcoming semester, his parents inadvertently converted what should have been *his* dilemma ("How do I get my parents to fund my return to school?") into *their* dilemma ("How do we get Alex to sit down and present us with his plans for the semester?"). They would have gotten further with something like "Before we write the check for your upcoming semester's tuition [most certainly their business], we'll need to hear from you about your plan for avoiding the difficulty you got into last semester. Let us know when you're ready to have that conversation." This would place the initiative and the dilemma where it belonged— in Alex's lap.

This may seem like I'm splitting hairs, but I can assure you once again that is not the case. The microstructure of any conversation reflects the underlying boundary paradigm of the parties involved. Most of us are acutely attuned to these underlying boundary paradigms. We sense when someone speaks to us in a patronizing or condescending manner, when someone "speaks down" to us, or when someone inquires about things that are none of their business. And if you and I have such finely tuned interpersonal radar in ordinary conversations, you can bet that your transitioner has his or her radar engaged when interacting with mom and dad.

The Secret Ingredient

Most effective parenting is a matter of applied common sense. When a child makes unwise choices, caring and concerned parents step in and do their best to redirect behavior. We advise, we teach, we insist. If necessary, we set up incentives and consequences. And if we're reasonably vigilant and consistent, our kids get the message and in time get themselves more or less on track.

Most of the time.

This book is about what happens when commonsense parenting no longer seems to work—when our children reach the age when our leverage and influence have diminished, and when our children, now old enough to make their own life choices and decisions, fail to take over the duties and responsibilities of "parenting" themselves toward adulthood.

What I've tried to show is that all is not lost when we find our transitioners struggling with the business of growing up and making a life for themselves. If you are willing to look at the subtle ways you may be perpetuating unrealistic adolescent thinking and expectations (chapter 7); if you are willing to reshape the boundaries of your relationship by changing your role from that of a supervisor-caretaker to that of a consultant (chapter 8); if you alter your strategies for encouraging motivation (chapter 9); if you can sort out financial support in a fashion that promotes rather than sabotages adult development (chapter 10); and if your communication patterns affirm and reinforce the adult status of your transitioner (chapter 11)—then it's reasonable to conclude that you are doing all you can to support the process of growing to adulthood.

But in all this there is a "secret ingredient," a lubricant that makes the gears of learning and maturation turn in the right direction. That ingredient, without which even your best efforts will likely come to naught, is *staying connected*. Over and over in my practice, I encounter frustrated and anguished parents who desperately love their struggling transitioners. But in these families, I often encounter transitioners who feel alienated and disconnected from these very same parents. I've worked in therapy with every sort of struggling transitioner imaginable—the immature, the anxious, the depressed, the drug- or alcohol-dependent, the self-absorbed, the impulsive, and the criminal—and if I had to put my finger on one factor above all others that points toward a promising prognosis, it would be the maintenance of a sense of emotional and empathic connection to their parents. This connection serves the transitioner the way an umbilical cord serves a fetus *in utero*; that connection is the conduit that enables transitioners to pick themselves up, to learn from their mistakes, and to find courage for the challenges of growing up.

Maintaining a nurturing emotional connection with someone who is neglecting responsibilities, making poor choices, mismanaging money, and sabotaging his or her future—this is the greatest challenge for parents of struggling transitioners. Virtually anything you attempt to do to help the situation— changing family culture, adjusting your expectations, revising the boundaries of your relationship, creating environmental circumstances conducive to motivation—will fall on rocky soil if your transitioner doesn't feel a sense of your love, acceptance, and understanding on a deeply personal level.

For most of the transitioners I see in my practice, the *fact* of their parents' love is not really an issue. They *know* their parents love them, whatever else might be going on in the relationship. At some point early in their therapy, I always ask this question: "Do your parents love you?" The answer is almost always yes. But I follow this with another question, one that I consider even more important: "*How do you know?* How does it come across to you?" I want to know if they have a *palpable experience* of their parents' love and acceptance—not in the abstract, but in the concrete interactions of their day-to-day lives. If the answer to this second question is empty, something like "I don't know; I guess I just know it," then we may have a problem. But when the answer is concrete and descriptive, something like "My dad and I have a favorite TV show" or "My mom laughs at my jokes," then I know the emotional umbilical cord is likely to be working just fine. The *fact* of loving your kids isn't enough. It's not enough that *you* know it. *They've* got to know it, and this means they've got to *feel* it from time to time in the give-and-take of your time together; they've got to *experience* it. Not all the time, of course, but enough to make your fundamental love, concern, and acceptance feel real.

I'm not naive. I know that it's difficult to commit yourself to a warm, playful, engaging moment of interaction when your transitioner is in the middle of flunking out of school or sleeping past noon or getting fired from another job. I also know full well that struggling transitioners often don't accept their parents' gestures of love and acceptance graciously. Frequently they are feeling so disappointed and angry with themselves that they can't imagine that you are feeling anything different. And to mitigate their presumption that you are rejecting them, they sometimes reject you first. My message is simple: Don't give up.

Whatever else you do, don't give up.

Recently I heard a radio interview with a mother whose twenty-seven-year-old daughter was a long-standing heroin addict. She told the story of her repeated attempts to rescue her daughter, setting up and funding multiple unsuccessful tours of drug rehab. Out of money and emotionally exhausted, she finally gave up. She gave up, that is, on her attempts to fix the drug addiction, but not on her daughter herself. As she told the story, she arranged to meet her daughter for breakfast one Sunday morning and announced, in a spirit of resignation and acceptance (rather than frustration and disappointment), that she was letting go of her focus on the drug addiction and wanted only to meet her daughter once a week for breakfast. She committed to spending this modicum of time together in order to stay connected. Her daughter agreed. Accepting that her daughter's drug addiction, for all the pain it caused, was *fundamentally her daughter's business* and that she wanted to stay connected to her daughter *regardless*, they began what became a Sunday-morning ritual.

At the end of the interview, this mother added, almost as an aside, that her daughter was then, at the time of the interview, once again in drug rehab. But for the first time, and certainly not by coincidence, she was there at her own initiative. I can't help but believe that those Sunday mornings together—and the daughter's palpable experience of her mother's desire to stay connected in spite of everything else—had a great deal to do with this young woman's decision to take on the challenge of growing up and assuming ownership of her life.

Chapter 12

Dear Twentysomething

A Letter to Your Struggling Transitioner

Dear Twentysomething,

I don't know you. I don't know your name. But let me introduce myself: I'm Mark McConville, and I've been talking to your parents. Possibly in person, but more likely through a book I wrote. The important thing for you to know is that I've spent hundreds of hours talking to parents like yours. I work with these parents—and wrote my book—to help them do a better job of getting along with their post-high-school twentysomething children.

In other words: *you.*

Here's what I think I know about you. You're probably somewhere between the ages of eighteen and thirty, and wrestling with how to get your parents to start treating you like an adult (or at least to stop treating you like a kid). You're also trying to get your life in gear.

And you're probably frustrated, annoyed, and irritated with all of it.

I don't blame you.

I also don't blame you if you're similarly frustrated, annoyed, and irritated at the fact that you've been handed this to read. Why? Because I'm guessing that someone (your parents, maybe, or a counselor) put this letter in your hands. I know that when someone puts something in *my* hands and says, "Here, read this," I usually smile politely, assure them I'll take a look at it, give it a glance, and then toss it in the nearest trash-can after they leave the scene.

I wouldn't blame you for doing the same thing, either.

But I have a different suggestion. Give me a few pages to capture your interest and to show you how things might be different (for example, maybe you wouldn't feel so frustrated, annoyed, and irritated, or maybe your parents could get off your back). If you don't find anything useful in these pages, then throw this in the trash. No hard feelings on my part; just good wishes for you to accomplish whatever it is you're up to.

■ ■ ■

Here's what I said to your parents in person or through the book, and what I advised them to do. In situations like yours, parents often get anxious and look for ways that they can be helpful. Some of the ways they try to help can be useful—such as putting a roof over your head or paying your rent or offering to pay for school. But sometimes their efforts can be annoying and intrusive, such as when they keep asking if you're looking for a job or whether you've requested more hours at work. Or maybe they complain when you stay out late or sleep in. If you're like a lot of twentysomethings living at home, your relationship with your parents has become strained. People like you often tell me that they feel judged by their parents, like they're a "disappointment." They also tell me that they *hate* that feeling.

I remember hating that feeling, too.

■ ■ ■

Here's how I'm trying to help. I told your parents to look at *their own* behavior in parenting and to begin treating you as an adult. I advised them to offer you *support*—their wisdom, their knowledge of how the world works, their financial help for important things like education and health care. But I also asked them to recognize that you are now the owner and manager of your life and your future. I asked them to begin thinking of you as someone with *your own* ideas and preferences and *your own* values and priorities—which may be different from theirs.

I also asked them to stop trying to *motivate* you. It drives me crazy when another person tries to motivate *me* to do something that's more *their* agenda than mine, so I assume it likely bothers you as well. Motivating *oneself* is a challenge that all people face at one time or another, but it's not a problem that anyone else can solve for you.

There's one other thing I told your parents: No matter what happens, no matter how badly you drop the ball or screw up, no matter what sort of shitshow your life becomes, they can *never* abandon you emotionally. You're their kid. They decided to have you. It doesn't matter if you're the valedictorian of your college class or an addict with a penchant for "borrowing" their credit cards; you're still their kid. They can never stop loving you, even if you're a complete pain in the ass. Never.

If your parents are like most whom I've met or worked with, they listened to what I told them. They're crazy about you even when you make them crazy. That's why, by the way, almost all parents are crazy and drive their children crazy: they love their sons and daughters so much that sometimes they can't see when their best intentions aren't helping. After I explain this, most parents calm down and start looking at how they can change.

In a nutshell, I told your parents to start thinking of you as an *adult*. In fact, you may already be noticing some changes in the way they treat and interact with you.

But now let's talk about *you*.

■ ■ ■

It turns out that your parents are probably only *half* the problem. A parent-child relationship—regardless of the age of the child or parent—is a sort of dance that evolves over time. The dance evolves from the parents being responsible for everything (early childhood), to sharing responsibility with a teenager (adolescence), to eventually having little or no responsibility for the full-grown child (adulthood).

Unfortunately, in some families—maybe yours—parents and children can *both* get stuck in the dance of adolescence, and neither can break free. Your parents do the dance by treating you like a teenager; you may do the dance by continuing to imitate one. My job is to show all of you how to escape this exhausting, irritating dance and to get your relationships—and your lives— back on track and on an adult footing.

But first things first. What does it mean to be an adult?

This takes longer and is far more complicated than most people realize. In the developed world, we don't magically become adults at age eighteen. In fact, the process takes much longer, typically stretching from high school graduation (usually around age eighteen) to the establishment of long-term commitments— such as a career, marriage, and children—usually somewhere in the thirties. Developmental psychologist Jeffrey Arnett calls this period of life *emerging adulthood.* You're not an adolescent anymore, but you're not (and you're not *supposed to be*) a full-fledged adult, either.

When Arnett asked twentysomethings what they considered to be the hallmarks of adulthood, they listed three things: making important life decisions, accepting real-life responsibilities, and attaining financial independence. But the most interesting thing he discovered was how long it takes to achieve these things: It's not until *they are twenty-six-and-a-half years old* that *half* of all people feel like an adult *half of the time!* And it's not until the late twenties that most people feel like an adult *most* of the time. (Forget about feeling like an adult *all* of the time; that never happens.)

Given all this, what are *you* supposed to do? Stay frustrated, annoyed, and irritated until you're thirty and hope everything works out?

There's a better way. In fact, there's a clear path to managing your personal transition into emerging adulthood. Every more or less successful adult you know has traveled this same path, whether they realize it or not or whether they talk about it or not. To navigate this path, you must confront *three* challenges that pave the way to a productive and satisfying adult life. These challenges are what psychologists call *developmental tasks*, things you must learn at a given stage of life to move on to the next one. And while you don't necessarily have to *master* these tasks of *emerging adulthood*, you do have to learn how to manage them well enough to move toward running your own life. Here they are:

Developmental Task 1

The first task is *becoming responsible*, which is likely very different from what you think it is, or from the topic on which your parents may be lecturing you. They and you may be stuck in thinking of you as being much younger, back when being responsible meant doing your homework, walking the dog, or taking out the trash—whatever you were expected to do. Being responsible in childhood basically means doing stuff adults want you to do.

That's not what I'm talking about.

For you, responsibility now means something completely different. It means *ownership*, as in taking ownership of your life. When you were in high school, adults set the framework and direction for your life. For example, state or national law said you had to attend school until a certain age. The adults in your life and you "co-owned" the responsibility for getting you ready for your future.

Things are different now. You own your future, whether you feel ready or not. By the way, if you don't feel ready—news flash—you're normal!

Taking ownership of your life is mostly a great improvement; you make your own choices and find the people and things that *you* like. It's exciting and liberating, but it comes at price. Ownership means you now have to manage the boring details that adults took care of when you were younger. Here's a hypothetical example. Let's say you are unlucky enough to have been born with diabetes. You don't deserve it, you didn't cause it, but you've got it. Bad luck. When you were younger, your parents owned the job of making sure your blood sugar stayed in the acceptable range; they monitored and managed your diet. You got used to their doing that; maybe you appreciated their oversight, or maybe it annoyed you. Either way, *you* didn't have to worry about it. But once you turned eighteen, it's as if they took the deed to your diabetes and signed it over to you. "Here, this belongs to you now! It's your responsibility to manage it. You own it."

In some ways, that sucks. But it's also part of the price for not feeling frustrated, annoyed, and irritated all the time with your parents and your life. There is a satisfaction in ownership of your life that can't be earned or enjoyed in any other way, and that makes increased responsibility not only tolerable but vital to your self-confidence and self-worth.

You probably don't have diabetes, but you certainly have other things to manage. Maybe you have ADHD. Or you tend to get depressed when things go badly. Or you're socially anxious or a procrastinator or have no idea what you want to do in life. Or you get embarrassed or intimidated when you apply for a job or interact with authority figures. Maybe you go a little overboard with alcohol or drug use.

In other words, you're human.

None of us is perfect, but all of us still have things to manage, like it or not. And one of the simple but critical things necessary for becoming and feeling like an adult—one of the *developmental tasks*—is owning your shit. That's what I mean by *responsibility*.

There's another type of responsibility, too, that may look insignificant on the surface, but is vitally important: *administrative responsibility*. Administrative responsibility has to do with all the pain-in-the-ass minutiae that must be managed to keep a life on track. I could give pages of examples. Paying a parking ticket by the deadline. Calling your dentist to reschedule an appointment. Getting your driver's license renewed. Going to the registrar's office at the community college to find out what payment plans are available. Filling out a job application, and then following up with a phone call or email. Getting your rent in on time. Checking the pressure of your tires before a road trip.

In short, administrative responsibility has to do with all the dreary planning and nuts and bolts of life that prevent bad things from happening to you. During your high school years, your parents probably took care of this stuff or else nagged until you managed it yourself, just to get them to get off your back.

Here's a question you might consider: *How good am I at managing these sorts of administrative responsibilities?* Don't feel bad, regardless of your answer. A huge percentage of twentysome-things are terrible at this. This often drives parents nuts, be-cause from their point of view, these small tasks are simple to perform and require little in the way of energy or expertise. Par-ents are almost always mystified when a twentysomething avoids or forgets a simple administrative responsibility. Surpris-ingly, their twentysomething is usually just as mystified as to why he avoids and neglects this stuff.

But why?

This mystery was solved for me by a twenty-one-year-old cli-ent of mine several years ago. Ben was home from college and needed a summer job. His father was a businessman, and he had arranged for one of his buddies to hire Ben. The only prob-lem was that Ben had to call to set up an interview, and he kept putting it off. His father nagged; Ben procrastinated. In the end, his father called the prospective employer and set up the meet-ing himself. Ben got the job and worked through the summer. Case closed, but still a mystery.

Fast-forward several months. Ben and I were talking about his plans for the fall semester when he offhandedly misspoke. "I'm going back several days early irregardless . . ." he began. "Wait, *irregardless*, is that a word?" he asked, followed by "Is it *irregardless* or *regardless*?"

"Regardless," I offered as Ben shook his head, visibly embar-rassed and flustered, far out of proportion to an innocuously misspoken word. "I *hate* when I do that," he sputtered. "When I was in high school, that never bothered me. I would just jive-talk myself around what I wanted to say. But I can't do that now. I try to sound like an adult, and I just feel so stupid when I don't know the word or say it wrong."

After a few moments, Ben looked up and said, "That's what that phone call was about, the one I didn't want to make. I was just so worried about saying something stupid, afraid he'd think, *This is just some kid!*"

I think Ben speaks for a lot of people. One of the hardest things about transitioning into emerging adulthood is that you're supposed to start passing yourself off as an adult—but you're still at an age when almost no one *feels* like an adult. People at this age often have a sense of faking it and a fear of not being taken seriously. This is the solution to the mystery of Ben's avoidance. Those simple administrative tasks that he and many other twentysomethings neglect and avoid are all things that *adults* do. And taking ownership of them can feel, in a subtle but powerful way, like stepping up and starting to think of yourself as an adult.

If you or someone you know avoids these seemingly simple forms of responsibility, it's probably because they symbolize something that's not simple at all. In fact, they symbolize something risky; something you may, deep down, fear that you're not ready for—*feeling like an adult*. Chances are, your parents felt the same way when they were your age. I certainly did.

Developmental Task 2

The second developmental task for twentysomethings is *finding a sense of direction*, which is as complicated as it sounds. When I consult with emerging adults, they often complain that they don't know what they want to do in life. Or if they do know what they'd like to do, they can't figure out how to get there. College students often say the same thing. They're nineteen or twenty, the time has come to declare a major, and they're freaked because they haven't figured out what their long-term career will be. Nobody knows at that age, of course, but many start to beat themselves up. They imagine and feel like they're behind their peers, thinking that they'll never figure out what they want to do and that adulthood is just a mirage on a distant horizon. In fact, when I meet with twentysomethings who are clinically depressed, it's often because they're in despair over the possibility of ever having a meaningful and rewarding future.

Yet research shows that, on average, people don't figure out what they're going to do for their adult work life until around age thirty. And it's not unusual for people to take even longer, waiting till age thirty-five or forty. That's why I always tell clients: Take a breath. You've got time. The twenties are *supposed* to be a period of exploration. Even in professions where people start their training early—doctors, architects, engineers, and so forth—most don't figure out what kind of doctor, architect, or engineer they're going to be until around age thirty.

Rule number one, then, is to give yourself time to explore.

What you *do* have to figure out in your twenties are two things: *What do you like? What are you good at?* If you're a college student, you've probably run into the school of thought that says *study something that will get you a good job.* I understand that; it can be good advice, especially if you're accumulating a mountain of college debt. It's especially good advice if you find a course of study in a highly employable field *that you like and that you're good at.* If you like and are good at computers or graphic arts or math or economics—you're golden. Great career paths. But what if what you like, and are good at, is poetry or philosophy or sports trivia or the history of hip-hop?

You're screwed, right?

Not necessarily.

I have two grown children. One is a successful lawyer; the other has an MBA and works for a Fortune 500 company. They're adults, and have found their paths. One studied English literature and Italian in college; the other one majored in classics, reading and translating ancient Latin and Greek. Even when they were in college, there weren't a lot of jobs out there for people who can translate Aeschylus or who can do literary analysis of novels written in Italian. But this was what they liked and were good at, and in the process of their college experience, both learned how to think, write, and problem-solve.

The real point is that when you choose a course of study or a line of work that you like and are good at, *you are more likely to commit to it and own it.* Like to write? Start writing for at least an hour every day, and sign up for a creative writing course at your local community college. Music? Take lessons, practice, and form a band. Work in a music store and join the musicians union. Save money, buy first-class recording equipment, and record in your basement.

A client recently told me that he intended to support himself with a YouTube channel. Like many in my generation, I didn't know what he was talking about.

I asked, "Okay, have you gotten started?"

He hadn't.

"What's holding you back?"

"My parents," he answered. So we got his parents into the office, and I helped him to negotiate a six-month deal through which they would fully support his YouTube project. At the end of six months, if he hadn't begun to make money or at least look like he was on the way to making money, he agreed to get a conventional job and begin paying a modest amount of rent. My point to him was this: Stop talking the talk and start walking the walk. Commit yourself to something that matters to you—and figure out a way to have a go at it. If you throw yourself into a dream and fail, it is much easier on you emotionally to walk away than to live the rest of your life knowing that you held back in fear.

Let me take a minute to summarize what I've said so far. I've described two important developmental tasks that will lead you out of your rut and carry you toward a much better, more independent, and satisfying life.

One: Accept responsibility for managing the nuts and bolts of your life and your health. You've spent the first two decades of your life in the passenger seat. Time to slide over into the driver's seat, even if doing so is a bit intimidating and you don't know exactly where you're headed.

Two: Accept responsibility for your future. Own it. Commit to preparing for it. You find college difficult and boring? So do many of your peers. Stop complaining and stick with it, because you need all the education you can tolerate. The only jobs you can find are low-level and uninteresting? Again, stick with it. Employment on a résumé equals experience, and experience opens the doors to more interesting, more meaningful, and better-paying work. Your task right now is to *start* the journey toward your future, not complete it.

Developmental Task 3

The third challenge involves relationships. Most people agree that part of becoming an adult means *becoming independent*. You have to learn to think for yourself, make important life decisions, and eventually make enough money to support yourself. But there's a common misunderstanding about how people achieve independence that leads to a paradox: Most people—and particularly emerging adults—mistakenly think that independence means you have to *do it by yourself.* Independence, they think, equals going it alone.

This is dead wrong.

The only way anyone develops independence is by developing relationships in which they receive support. That's the secret sauce: Learning how to find and accept support is the only path to true independence. There's another corresponding paradox, too: Real-world, real-life independence isn't actually independence at all. It's *interdependence.* It's forming relationships in which you know you have people in your corner. People who are rooting for you, people who accept you the way you are, people who know you're anxious or flaky or insecure or grandiose or lazy or impulsive or a little crazy—and yet they accept you anyway. This is a universal human need: We need to be *known* and to be *accepted for who we are*. This is, of course, easier said than done, but if you don't currently have this in your life, it's time to find it. Look for friendships with peers who have depth and heart and emotions and understanding. Why? Because they're going through the same stage of life as you are, and it's easier to walk a new path with good companions.

Friendships with depth, genuine communication, and acceptance are one of the keys to developing independence.

There's more.

You also need to learn how to get support from people who are older, wiser, more informed, and more experienced that you. Think Luke Skywalker and Obi-Wan Kenobi; Frodo and Gandalf; Harry Potter and Rubeus Hagrid. There's a reason that stories of heroes coming of age always include a mentor, and that's because you can't figure out everything by yourself. It just doesn't work that way.

The challenge is that it's not always easy to find a mentor who knows exactly what you need to learn and who's willing to take you on as a pupil. In real life, you have to look for mentorship, and it probably won't be just one individual. It's going to be a bunch of people, and they'll show up at different times in your life. I found a golf pro who took me under his wing when I was seventeen, a psychology professor who did the same when I was twenty-one, and a psychiatrist colleague when I was twenty-seven. And then again, there was a remarkably wise therapist I saw in my early thirties. These people don't come knocking on your door. You have to go searching for them. But even more basic than getting lucky and finding the kind of mentor you'll remember for a lifetime is that you have to develop the skill of figuring out *who* knows more about something than you and then summon the courage to ask "stupid questions" (which means the *real* questions—the ones you don't yet know the answer to).

So the first part of building new relationships is to work at developing connections with peers in which you know and care enough about one another to enable you to turn to one another for understanding, support, and advice. The second part is learning how to procure support—encouragement, wisdom, advice, and knowledge—from people who know *more* about life than you do.

There's a third part, too, and that's straightening things out with your parents. Many of the twentysomethings I see in my practice complain about how their parents nag or don't have faith in them or try to run their lives or just radiate disapproval. In practice and in my book, I talk to parents—including yours—about owning their part of the problem, acknowledging that sometimes their efforts to be "helpful" aren't really helpful at all.

A lot of twentysomethings I see in counseling complain that their parents treat them like children, and they're often right. I make a point of talking to the parents about that, just as I did with your parents. I coach them in lots of ways to interact with you on a more adult-to-adult basis. One of my primary concerns is that they respect your boundaries, which means to get clearer about what's your business and what's their business. While they have every right to manage their own legitimate business (for example, having house rules that allow them to be comfortable in their own home), they should stay out of your business unless you invite them in. That's my message for parents. But here's my message for you: *If you want your parents to stay out of your business, you have to learn to manage your business in a way that doesn't require them to get involved.*

■ ■ ■

That's all I've got. That's my message. Becoming an adult is harder than most of us ever want to acknowledge, and far more difficult than anyone dares to tell you in high school. It's scary because nobody knows how to do it until they've already gone though it, and those with experience (including parents) often act as if it was no big deal or have forgotten their own struggles or don't want to admit their own insecurities and anxieties, whether from then or now.

I wish more people talked openly about this, but they don't.

As I said at the start, I don't know you, so I can't know what you're feeling, or why your parents bought my book or came to see me. But I have some guesses. Along with feeling frustrated, annoyed, and irritated, you may also be feeling stalled in life or worried that you're somehow not ready for adulthood. If you're like many twentysomethings I've worked with, you don't want to admit any of this to anyone. If we could talk, I would tell you this: Most of them feel the same way. Your parents felt the same way, too. You aren't alone, and you aren't broken. You're human, and this is the crooked path we each follow to our quirky, imperfect, rewarding futures.

So be afraid, but know that you will get through. The more honest you are with yourself about this, the better off you'll be.

■ ■ ■

I have a dear friend who dreamed of becoming a writer most of his life. He zigzagged through high school, college, and jobs he hated until he eventually leveraged his English degree and some freelance writing into a low-paying job at a small-time business magazine. He was in his early thirties, with a child on the way. He doesn't dwell on his story, but I know for a fact that he busted his ass and did the best job he could. He liked writing, and that job gave him an opportunity to write. Not what he *wanted* to write, but writing nonetheless. And then he got hired at a big-time business magazine, where after busting his ass some more and several promotions, he became editor in chief. Not his dream job, but closer to his dream.

My friend morphed from an adolescent high schooler to an English major to the editor of a magazine. He is presently the owner and CEO of a global management research company and is a sought-after speaker for business conferences. He's good at it, and it pays the bills.

The best part of his story, though, is this: He's now a writer, and he writes what he *wants* to write about. His recent publications include a major business book, a children's book (don't ask; the explanation would take pages), and he has another nonfiction book and a work of fiction in the hopper.

He's doing what he loves. But depicting his career would be like describing the path of someone scaling a climbing wall: Find your first foot support, then your first handhold. Hang on; you're holding on to the new support, but it's also holding you. And then look for the next navigable blocks on the wall. Go up, sideways, up, sideways again, maybe down a step, up, stretch, push hard. Take it one perilous step and handhold, one challenge at a time. You're scared of falling—it's a long way down, and there aren't any ropes on this wall—but you focus intently on the path. Breathe. Don't look down.

This is how it works; this is how lives and careers move forward. It's a climbing wall, not a highway.

■ ■ ■

So let me tell you what I love about this guy, my friend, the one who pursued his dream, climbed that unmapped vertical wall, and found his future self (and this is the mostly deeply guarded secret about growing up—the one most adults are either unwilling or unable to tell).

We're on the golf course together; it's late November in northeastern Ohio and no one else is on a golf course anywhere within fifty miles, because it's cold and wet and winter is just around the corner. We're walking side by side in relative silence, carrying our golf bags, and he turns to me and he says, "Dude, aren't you glad we never completely grew up?"

And my answer, of course, is . . .

"Yes, I am."

Good luck,

Mark McConville

Afterword

A Hard-Won Crown

S ome people move gracefully from adolescence through emerging adulthood, becoming full-fledged adults with productive lives and making the world a better place. Lots of people in my life fit this description. They were self-organizers and self-managers from a young age. Some people are blessed this way.

Others are less well equipped and prepared. These are typically kids whose capacity for organization and self-management is less well developed, or who may be more vulnerable to feeling anxious about challenges and embarrassed about stumbles. Or both.

■ ■ ■

I was one of those kids.

■ ■ ■

When my mother was dying, many years ago, she entrusted me with her personal journal (as an adult, I had adopted the role of family historian). Here is a fragment from that journal, written by her when I was twelve years old:

> All I hope to accomplish with this child is to make him responsible for his scheduled jobs—his practice and homework. He knows what he must do—he knows what time he should do them, but "forgets." Sometimes it's downright discouraging—I figure he'll never come through and develop that lovely sense of responsibility that his older brother was born with—a gift free and clear. So if and when Mark develops it, it will be a hard-won crown.

Today I wear that hard-won crown.

■ ■ ■

I experienced many of the challenges that your struggling transitioner is no doubt experiencing today. I was anxious, underachieving, unsure of myself, disorganized, forgetful, and embarrassed about making mistakes. But *I made it through*, and in no small measure due to my parents—who allowed me to make mistakes, provided guidance and support when I was open to it, encouraged me to follow my dreams and find my own path, and somehow, without ever saying the words out loud, let me know that they had my back, no matter what. My point is this: *You matter.* You can be the difference between your child's growing up or stalling out in recycled adolescence. Your love and support, your willingness to step back and allow your child to make mistakes and learn from them—and then being available in the aftermath *not* with "I told you so," but instead with "How can I help?"—that's what your struggling transitioner needs from you.

Growing up requires two essential things: time and love. Give them time. Give them love.

And have faith.

Appendix

Getting Professional Help

Failure to Launch was written for parents whose transitioners are failing to grow toward adulthood largely on account of *mild to moderate* degrees of anxiety, depression, substance use, and immaturity. If your emerging adult's situation is more severe—that is to say, his or her development is significantly impaired by cognitive dysfunction, psychiatric disorder, or substance abuse and addiction—you can benefit by getting yourself and your struggling transitioner professional support. Here are some options.

Individual Psychotherapy for Your Transitioner

This is appropriate and potentially helpful under certain conditions (but not others). If your transitioner *acknowledges and owns* his or her difficulties—as opposed to denying personal responsibility and blaming others—then he or she is likely to be an excellent candidate for individual therapy. The best way to find a good therapist is to ask professionals who regularly refer young adults to therapy—pediatricians, college or university mental health counseling services (they usually know who the good private therapists are in their vicinity), guidance counselors at private schools (these folks refer often and are discerning critics of the counseling services their students receive). Therapists who work effectively with adolescents typically do a good job working with struggling twentysomethings as well.

If your emerging adult is a college student wrestling with stress and its related symptomatology, most college campuses provide counseling and related mental health resources for students. If your college student is a do-it-yourselfer, you might recommend HeartMath Institute's stress management handbook: store.heartmath.org/store/teens/College-De-Stress-Handbook .html

If your transitioner does *not* have insight or take ownership of his or her difficulties, individual psychotherapy is not likely to be productive. If this is the case, you will likely derive more benefit from family therapy and/or parent guidance.

Family Therapy

For most of the cases in *Failure to Launch*, I employed a model that utilizes individual counseling with the transitioner, parent guidance and coaching for parents, and occasional joint sessions for both. Unfortunately, this is not the most common intervention model for struggling transitioners. Standard mental health practice most often offers treatment appropriate to a transitioner's *chronological* age rather than his or her developmental age and the "age" of their relational paradigm with parents. Since twenty-two-going-on-sixteen-year-olds are legally adults, many therapists refuse contact with parents. A common mistaken belief among mental health professionals is that including parents in the treatment process only contributes to treating their client like a child. To the contrary, I have found that involving parents in the therapy allows me to constructively influence the relationship dynamics in support of growth and development.

When I receive a referral for a twentysomething, my first order of business (usually through a phone or email conversation prior to scheduling) is to assess whether this individual is coming to me as an *adult* (self-referral, and capable of reflective ownership of issues and problems) or as an *"adolescent"* (coming at parents' urging or insistence, with insufficient ownership of his or her personal role in current difficulties, and with a strained parent-child relationship as part of the picture). In the latter case, I insist, matter-of-factly, upon meeting parents and transitioner together for the initial meeting—where I am able to get a better handle on how best and with whom to intervene in the particular situation. It might surprise some mental health practitioners to learn that transitioners rarely object to their parents' involvement in an initial meeting. And when I promise to help improve their relationship at home, transitioners are almost always interested. If you have a transitioner who is not a good candidate for individual therapy, I recommend trying to find someone who will work with you as a family. Also, this is an easier sell for your transitioner: make it clear that the purpose of consulting a professional *isn't* to fix him or her. It's to fix the *relationship*.

Parent Guidance and Support

If you are unable to get your son or daughter involved in an appropriate mental health or chemical dependency treatment regimen, *please* get some support for yourself. In doing so, make sure you see someone who is familiar with emerging adults and their developmental challenges. Emerging adulthood is a new specialization in the field of mental health. The other step parents can take when coping with a dysfunctional adult child is to find a support group, such as those sponsored by the National Alliance on Mental Illness (NAMI) or Al-Anon (when substance use/abuse in the issue). I have had numerous client parents who found such support groups invaluable.

Here is a link to a wonderful article in *Psychology Today* by Victoria Maxwell on how to respond to an adult child who refuses help for mental illness: www.psychologytoday.com/us/blog/crazy-life/201202/families-falling-apart-when-adult-children-mental-illness-dont-want-help

Chemical Dependency Programs

Whether your child is asking for help with substance use, abuse, or dependency, or you are insisting upon substance abuse intervention as a condition of continued material support, the necessary place to start is with an objective evaluation by a chemical dependency specialist. When I refer someone for evaluation, I use a local professional who has her own independent practice. I prefer her because she is *not* attached to a specific program. This allows her to be more objective in her assessment, as her singular focus is on the needs of the client, with no conflict of interest to meet the needs of an employer to fill treatment slots. As an independent specialist, she also has her thumb on the pulse of various treatment options in our area. Try to find a similar professional in your vicinity.

Residential Treatment Programs

These exist, are expensive, and vary greatly in specialization and quality. If you're looking in this direction, I recommend contacting a treatment program placement professional. There are many such placement professionals. These are two I've had good experience with:

Dr. Andrew Erkis: www.stratasconsultinggroup.com/andrew-erkis

Dr. Carol Maxym: www.maxymconsulting.com

If you prefer to start by doing some research into treatment programs on your own, here's a website that serves as a portal to many such treatment programs: www.allkindsoftherapy.com /treatment/youngadults/residential-treatment

■ ■ ■

Think back to chapter 5, where I emphasized the need for transitioners to learn how to seek out *support*, from peers, mentors, and parents. I'm advising you the same thing. Reach out and get yourself some support. Reading this book was a step in that direction. Don't stop here.

Acknowledgments

Over a million books are published every year, so one more or less isn't that big a deal in the overall scheme of things. That doesn't change the fact that writing a book is exciting, challenging, terrifying, bewildering, frustrating, and fulfilling. And certainly the most rewarding part of the entire enterprise is having an opportunity to acknowledge the people who mean so much to me and have been so encouraging and supportive along the way. Publishing a book is a fairly public form of sticking your neck out into a contemporary world rife with disparagement and negativity. Anyone willing to venture into that terrain with less than prodigious relational support is, frankly, nuts.

Two things I can confidently say about myself: I'm not nuts; and I've been the benefactor of prodigious amounts of relational support.

First and foremost, always, I want to acknowledge my dearest friend, partner, love of my life, and spouse of the last half century, Joanne Kaucic McConville, whose effortless integrity and uncompromising grace have grounded and inspired me all these years. Without her influence, I certainly would never have come to write this book. And my children—Luke Francis McConville and Meghan Hayes McConville Hale—who, whether they wish to bear the burden, make this whole business of living add up and make sense, and their spouses, Mary Beth Cook McConville and David Hale, who have generously welcomed us into their families. And to their children, Conor Anthony, Rory Collins, Patrick Finn, Mary Janet, Clara McConville, Annie Susanna, and Maia McKenna, I wish to say: You're it! The whole story. With you, I finally understand Piaget's joy: Grandparenting is life's ultimate reward.

In addition, I wish to acknowledge:

. . . the Arcadians Writers Group, whose members Ed Walsh and Jim Wood have been the source of ongoing support and inspiration.

. . . the many readers of parts or all of the manuscript, particularly Anne van de Waal, Dr. William O'Neil, and Emma Brandt (who, despite her protestations, is a rock star).

. . . Bronagh Starrs, the best practicing adolescent therapist on the planet; and Gordon Wheeler, whose brilliant writing and theorizing have been my North Star for many years.

. . . members of my ongoing psychotherapy peer consultation group, whose members Barbara Fields, Heidi Abrams, and Marlene Blumenthal, together with our inspirational mentor Frances Baker, collectively bring to the table almost two centuries of professional experience. Thank you for the encouragement, guidance, insight, and continued learning we have shared with one another all these years.

. . . the extraordinary faculties and staffs of Hathaway Brown School and University School, who are single-mindedly devoted to the growth and development of young people, and the faculty of the Gestalt Institute of Cleveland, who have played an important role in my own growth and development.

. . . David Granoff, Psy.D., and Denise Hodson, R.N.—deeply respected and inspirational colleagues, and Mark Warren, M.D., compadre, confidant, and unfailing source of support.

. . . my agent, Gail Ross, of Ross-Noon, and my editor, Michelle Howry, of Putnam/Penguin Random House, who are, in the apt words of my dear friend and colleague Lisa Damour, "smart in ways we psychotherapists never dreamed of." And to Lisa herself, my dear friend and brilliant colleague, who saw possibilities in my manuscript that I did not see myself, and who, in the true spirit of mentorship, walked me along the path, generously sharing her practical experience and professional wisdom. Without Lisa's support, this book would never have launched.

. . . my fellow associates of the MGL Golfing Society—Mike Gassman, Christian Bernadotte, Rick Bauchard, Bill Plesec, Bill Better, Lee Hooper, and Ken Butze—who ensure that I will never take myself too seriously. And finally, my fellow golf obsessive, writer, amateur philosopher, humorist, and confidant, John Brandt, without whose incisive feedback and wild optimism this manuscript would likely have been locked in a desk drawer or found the bottom of some editor's trash can, and whose perspective continues to remind me that adulthood, for all it's cracked up to be, is not the last word.

Bibliography

Brown, Brené. *The Gifts of Imperfection: Let Go of Who You Think You're Supposed to Be and Embrace Who You Are*. Center City, MN: Hazelden, 2010.

Kaufman, Gershen. *The Psychology of Shame: Theory and Treatment of Shame-Based Syndromes*. New York: Springer, 1989.

Kegan, Robert. *The Evolving Self: Problem and Process in Human Development*. Cambridge, MA: Harvard University Press, 1982.

———. *In Over Our Heads: The Mental Demands of Modern Life*. Cambridge, MA: Harvard University Press, 1994.

Lahey, Jessica. *The Gift of Failure: How the Best Parents Learn to Let Go So Their Children Will Succeed*. New York: Harper Paperbacks, 2016.

Lancy, David F. *Raising Children: Surprising Insights from Other Cultures*. New York: Cambridge University Press, 2017.

Lee, Robert G., and Gordon Wheeler, eds. *The Voice of Shame: Silence and Connection in Psychotherapy*. San Francisco: Jossey-Bass, 1996.

Levinson, Daniel J. *The Seasons of a Man's Life*. New York: Knopf, 1978.

Marcel, Gabriel. *Homo Viator: Introduction to a Metaphysic of Hope*. Emma Craufurd, trans. New York: Harper Torchbooks, 1962.

McConville, Mark. *Adolescence: Psychotherapy and the Emergent Self*. San Francisco: Jossey-Bass, 1995.

Pink, Daniel H. *Drive: The Surprising Truth About What Motivates Us*. New York: Riverhead Books, 2009.

Robine, Jean-Marie. *On the Occasion of an Other*. Gouldsboro, ME: Gestalt Journal Press, 2011.

Sheehy, Gail. *Passages: Predictable Crises of Adult Life*. New York: E. P. Dutton, 1976.

Wheeler, Gordon. *Beyond Individualism: Toward a New Understanding of Self, Relationship, and Experience*. Hillsdale, NJ: GIC Press, distributed by the Analytic Press, 2000.

Yalom, Irvin D. *Existential Psychotherapy*. New York: Basic Books, 1980.

Index

About the Author

Mark McConville, Ph.D., is a clinical psychologist in private practice in Beachwood, Ohio, specializing in adult, adolescent, emerging adult, and family psychology. Dr. McConville is a senior faculty member at the Gestalt Institute of Cleveland, and has published and taught widely on the subjects of adolescent and emerging adult development, parenting, and counseling methodology.

His book *Adolescence: Psychotherapy and the Emergent Self* (Jossey-Bass, 1995) was awarded the 1995 Nevis Prize for Outstanding Contribution to Gestalt Therapy theory. He is the author of the *Counseling Feedback Report*, an innovative and widely used adolescent assessment tool, and is coeditor of *The Heart of Development: Gestalt Approaches to Childhood and Adolescence*, vols. I & II (The Analytic Press, 2001). Additionally, Dr. McConville has published a dozen articles in peer review journals, and taught internationally on the subjects of development and psychotherapy and the contribution of existential-phenomenology to the practice of Gestalt therapy.

In addition to his private clinical practice, Dr. McConville serves as consulting psychologist to Hathaway Brown School and University School, both in the Cleveland area. He lives in Shaker Heights, Ohio, with his wife, and within visiting distance of his two adult children and seven grandchildren.